MY CHILDREN, MY HEROES

MEMOIRS OF A HOLOCAUST MOTHER

By
Sonia Minuskin

**Translated and Annotated by Her Son,
Harold Minuskin**

Cover: Sonia (Shanke) Orlinsky Minuskin, ca. early 1930s.
Cover photo courtesy of Carl Minuskin.

My Children, My Heroes
Memoirs of a Holocaust Mother

Translated and Annotated by
Her Son, Harold Minuskin

Library of Congress

ISBN: 978-1-60743-692-8
First Edition

Printed in the United States of America
2009
by Allegra Printing & Imaging, Prescott, Arizona

In loving memory of
Sonia (Shanke) Orlinsky Minuskin
for her courageous struggle to save her children.

May her memory live on forever.

MY CHILDREN, MY HEROES
MEMOIRS OF A HOLOCAUST MOTHER

Contents

PART I: MY CHILDREN, MY HEROES
Memoirs of a Holocaust Mother

PART II: TRANSLATOR'S MEMORIES
Aftermath of the War

Back In Time – Through A Child's Eyes   90

PART III: A TRIBUTE TO SHLAMKE MINUSKIN AND HIS NEPHEW, KALMAN MINUSKIN

PART IV: THE ZHETLER PARTISANS ORGANIZE AND FIGHT BACK: THE MISSIONS

PREFACE

Over the six-month period it took me to translate from Yiddish to English my mother's story of survival, my own recollections were rekindled. As I read and re-read each page of my mother's handwritten Yiddish text, I was carried back in time to relive the experiences that had become a cloudy memory. The seriousness of the life and death struggle in my small town and our escape into the Belorussian forest was buried within me.

It was not until the 1980s before I could emotionally prepare myself to read and experience my mother's heroic struggle for survival, not only for herself but for her two small children – my younger brother and me. This was a time and place in history when most families suffered the loss of their children from starvation, disease, and exposure to the cold Russian winters, or at the hands of the Germans and their collaborators.

As I worked to complete this translation, I was extremely careful to use her own words as she wrote them. Since she wrote her memoirs from about 1945 to 1948, some parts may appear disjointed. To bridge the gap, I have included information provided to me by the extended family of survivors of our town, plus my own childhood memories.

We were fortunate to have a mother that always cared for our well-being. My great disappointment was that my dear mother was not with us when this book was published. She died peacefully on November 7, 2008. She was 102 years old. I dedicate this book to her memory.

Harold Minuskin

ACKNOWLEDGEMENTS

I would like to acknowledge the help of my brother, Carl, for his invaluable assistance and for providing some of the photographs that helped make this book a reality. I also want thank my wife, Arlene, who spent countless hours reading, making suggestions and editing the manuscript.

I would like to give thanks to Sasha Mednikov for his translation of the Russian documents. Rabbi William L. Berkowitz was also very helpful with the translation of the Hebrew captions of photographs from the book, *Zhetel Our Town*, and other sources. Although these photographs were not used in this book, they provided important historical information.

A very special posthumous thanks to my cousin, Kalman Minuskin, who provided me the accounts of Zhetel Partisan missions before he passed away.

To my good friends, Richard and Joanne Brody and Francine Garner, thank you for your encouragement, moral support and belief in the importance of sharing my mother's extraordinary story with others.

Harold Minuskin

TRANSLATOR'S INTRODUCTION

These are the memoirs of a mother's struggle to survive with her two young sons in a time when the Nazi Third Reich was at its most powerful, in the process of terrorizing, brutalizing and murdering six million European Jews. It is the account of my mother, *Shanke* (Sonia) Orlinsky Minuskin, born in the small *shtetl* (town) of Zhetel, Poland (later part of Belorussia), the youngest of six siblings, and how she came to terms with fear, hunger, bitter cold, and the most inhumane of conditions. It is her story in her own words of how she survived the Holocaust and saved her two young children. Her motives and determination are inspirational given the events that she was forced to live through.

Life for the Jewish population throughout Europe in the early twentieth century was harsh, dangerous and often times fatal. Discrimination against Jewish people was ingrained in the gentile population. The State and its institutions sponsored and supported anti-Semitism. Over many years, extremely violent and barbaric organized persecutions and massacres called *pogroms* resulted in many Jewish deaths. This left the Jewish population physically and psychologically wounded, never knowing what would happen to them at any given time.

With the rise of Nazism in Germany in the 1930s, came the Third Reich, the Gestapo, the SS (an elite quasi-military unit of the Nazi party), and a militaristic, war mongering, sadistic anti-Semitic fascist dictatorship.

Following the death in May 1935 of Marshal Jezef Pilsudski, the president of the Polish Republic, the rise of Hitler and the fate of Germany's Jews gave way to a sense of deep concern by the 3.5 million Jews in Poland. The feeling was that Marshal Pilsudski's leadership had been the last to curb Poland's existing anti-Semitism, which would now flourish unchecked. A number of events validated that belief. Zalman Lubetski, a Jew who was serving in the Polish Fifth Infantry Regiment, was told by his anti-Semitic comrades: "Your grandfather is dead; there is no longer anyone in Poland to protect you." With Pilsudski dead, there was de facto official approval for anti-Jewish activity.[1]

During the years 1935-1937, there were a number of anti-Jewish pogroms in Poland. There was one is Grodno in 1935, then in Przytyk and Minsk-Mazowieck in 1936, and in Czestochowa, Bszesc and Begiem in 1937.[1]

In November 1938, *Kristallnacht*, the Night of Broken Glass, the worst pogrom targeting Jewish citizens in the history of Germany, took place with the total support and approval of the Nazi Third Reich. It was a night of horror for Jewish people throughout Germany. Synagogues, Jewish homes and Jewish shops were targeted, ransacked and set on fire. Many Jewish men, women and children able to escape the flames were shot.

Kristallnacht and its aftermath marked a major turning point and escalation of Nazi persecution of the Jewish people. Harsh and brutal measures continued, and within days thousands of Jewish families were rounded up and sent to concentration camps. It marked the beginning of the systematic eradication of a people who could trace their ancestry in Germany to Roman times, and served as a prelude to the Holocaust that was to follow.

Ten months after Kristallnacht, in September 1939, the armies of Germany's Nazi Third Reich invaded Poland. The objective was the expansion of territories, conquest of Poland and Russia and the elimination of the entire Jewish population in Europe. With the conquest of Poland, the German army, along with the Gestapo and the SS, were free to terrorize and sadistically murder innocent Polish Jews. The systematic Nazi progression of persecution, genocide and ethnic cleansing climaxed with the murder of six million Jewish people. Many of these Jews spoke Yiddish and were schooled in the Talmud, the basis of religious authority in Orthodox Judaism.

The ability to survive the Holocaust was a monumental task. This is the story of my mother, of how she not only survived, but more important to her, how she was able to save the lives of her two small sons. Her task was to evade capture and endure the legendary long bitter cold Russian winters while trying to find food, medical help, clothing, and shelter for herself and her two small children. Her challenge was to overcome the horrors and hardships surrounding her, while avoiding instant death if captured.

The survivors of the Nazi massacres, who sought refuge in the forests of Belorussia, were exposed to the cruelest and most unforgiving primitive conditions. Life was especially vulnerable during the harsh Russian winters. These cruel and savage conditions continued not for a few months, but dragged on for years in these forests. The years of Nazi terror was an experience in hell on earth that had no equal. Insomnia, tormenting nightmares and pain and are just a few of the unbearable scars that plagued my mother long after World War II ended.

While many stories have emerged about the Nazi concentration camps, other stories exist about the determined survival and heroism of Jews who fought against the German murderers and their collaborators. Those of us who survived the massacres fled into the nearby forests and lived in hiding during the war years. Young men and women joined with the partisans and fought courageously against the German occupiers, extracting revenge on the German murderers at every opportunity. The Russian Army wisely parachuted officers into the area in which the Jewish partisans were located and provided leadership and supplies to mount organized battles against the German occupiers.

I have included a section as a tribute to my cousin, Kalman Minuskin, and his extraordinary struggle for survival and heroism. Kalman was in hiding with my family and later joined the partisans at the age of 12. There is also a tribute to my father that documents his bravery to save the lives of Kalman's mother and brother during the German roundup of Jews and their immediate massacre.

To underscore the successful Jewish partisan resistance against their German occupiers, several detailed battles are described. The accounts of victorious battles and fierce combat waged by the Jewish partisans against the Germans were derived from Kalman's book, *In the Ghetto and In the Forest*, and another reference. The stories of partisan reprisal missions against informers who were responsible for the deaths of countless Jews are also described in these books.[2, 3, 4]

Some of my own memories are included from the perspective of a three to seven year old child who lived in hiding in the forests for two and a half years. I would not remember what a normal home looked like until we were liberated.

Our family once lived in Zdienciol, Poland, located near the Belorussian border. The Yiddish name of our town was called

Zhetel. Its name and jurisdiction, whether Polish or Russian, varied, depending on the political posture of the times. The former Polish name of Zdienciol has been replaced by its Russian name, Dyatlovo, and is now part of Belarus.

In our town, many languages were spoken, but we spoke primarily Yiddish. Throughout the book I have chosen to use our Yiddish names: my mother is *Shanke*, which in Yiddish means beautiful; my father is *Shlamke*; I am *Henikel*; my brother is *Kalmanke*. Both my brother and I were named after our two grandfathers. When we came to America we tried to conform as all refugees did at the time. My mother chose Sonia as her Americanized name; my father became Sam; I would be called Harold; and my brother was named Carl.

Yiddish, Hebrew and Russian words, plus other languages, are written in *italics*, and included in Appendix C. My own annotations are also in italics, followed by my initials, H.M.

My mother's memoirs were hand-written by her in Yiddish. In 1992, she recorded them into a cassette recorder, also in Yiddish. At the time, she was still in good health and was of clear mind. I used this recording and the original Yiddish text as references for an accurate translation, as parts of the text were obscured by time and difficult to read.

Harold Minuskin

PART I

MY CHILDREN, MY HEROES

MEMOIRS OF A HOLOCAUST MOTHER

THE GERMAN OCCUPATION OF ZHETEL

I am more than certain that this language is too poor or inadequate to write and to tell you what I went through with my dear ones in the days that I was separated from you. It was in the year 1939 when the Germans first entered our small town of Zhetel. A black cloud covered all our hearts. We knew that no good occurrences await us. That what they did to us we never expected.

(My mother's following recollections cover a period of many months. – H.M.)

Every day more hardships were created. With heavy hearts we walked about. We hoped to God that we did not do anything that made us guilty of such treatment. We heard news from nearby towns and villages about what the Germans had already done.

Every day became harder and darker for us. The Germans began by asking us for all our goods and possessions. Without reservations, we obeyed all their orders. I remember the order that appeared in the market place that Jews do not have the right to walk on the sidewalk, and Jews don't have a right to

1

ride in a conveyance such as in a wagon, train, car, or bus. Jews must wear a yellow Star of David.

The Jews with yellow patches on their backs, with drawn faces, were scared, afraid, bewildered and hungry. God in heaven, why are we deserving of this? Our elders and the younger people fasted with the hope that God will have pity on those innocents that don't know why the Germans are cutting our throats and slaughtering us.

My dear ones, how sad it is to see you every day before my eyes. On such nice days I *bahynk* (long) for you. On such days our nice people, *balabosteym* (homemakers), our dear and close ones, ran aimlessly back and forth out of breath during those tragic days. What more can I write?

◊ ◊ ◊

The situation became worse from day to day. We start to speak about taking revenge and about who will be able to take revenge on our behalf.

Each day there are new orders. The day we were driven into the ghetto, we all were to be in a place on one street. We had only three hours to accomplish the move. It meant that all 4000 of us would have to be located on this one street. I will never forget the panic of the small children in the laps of their mothers, all crying as to where shall they go and what shall they do. Jews with clasped hands understood what was happening, were saying prayers in small corners of that one street and remained sitting.

Trouble began when you left the ghetto to buy something. You would surely give your life if you took or received any goods over the gate that we were all gathered in. We had to eat from rations of six ounces of margarine, thin pieces of cheese and very little bread. Epidemics broke out from hunger, from the filth and from the *eingshaft* (crowded conditions) of people.

We walked around in a daze, contemplating meeting each other in heaven. We spoke about finding a syringe or a poison that would bring us instant death. As we talked about this, the question was where could we find such things. Maybe we can choke ourselves. First the children, or first the adults?

Our brothers sat in a cordoned off box surrounded by barbed wire. They sat there day and night and were not able to sleep. They searched their minds what to do, how do we save ourselves. But the Germans were very strict and the Jews lost any hope.

Each one of us from our village began to build a hiding place (in the ghetto) during the middle of the night. The hiding places were built under a stall, in a cellar, in an attic. They ripped at the earth with their bare hands and nails; they wanted to live. We will have revenge on the bloody murderers. God in Heaven, who among is blessed? Hunger, sickness and overcrowding had ruined our nice small village. Blackened with dirt, bitterness, and nervousness made it so that no one spoke to each other. Peasants (non-Jews) who would enter the Jewish ghetto would take Jewish possessions. They would say to the Jews in the ghetto "you will be killed anyway."

A peasant came to me and asked for my beds. I owned two nickel beds. He says, "Why do you need the beds, you won't live for long; maybe one day or two? You can in the meantime sleep on the floor." Such visitors came to take our possessions while we were still alive. This happened to each one of us. So our hopes faded with the harsh words of our peasant neighbors.

(As my mother dictated in Yiddish her written text into the cassette recorder, and thinking that the microphone was off, she asks me, "Do you understand what the goiyem (gentiles) did to us?" – H.M.)

Any hopes we had disappeared. Crying did not help. One mother who had children was not able to look at the tragedy that awaited us. She was stone faced; she did not speak: she was bitter, sitting and crying all the time. You could not recognize her.

My dear friends, I won't forget my impressions of your expressions from the *frehlache* (happy) days. And now the bitter day has arrived that I had to part with my loving and *klugeh* (wise) mother. I will never forget the words we spoke at the time.

(My mother does not go into the details of the words that she spoke with her mother, my grandmother. Nor does my mother explain why she was separated from her mother at this time. – H.M.)

MASS GRAVES AND HIDING PLACES

It was one day before the first of May. It was raining in the evening when we heard a car arrive at the police station. We

4

found out that orders were received to dig a ditch that was 100 feet long and 60 feet wide. It was to be dug outside the village in an area forbidden to Jews. To get there, people had to be driven in trucks. We later found out that the Germans had made plans to kill half the population of our village, mostly the elderly and the children. The Germans hired nearby peasants to dig the large ditch.

We are all sitting stone faced, bewildered; others walk about wrenching their hands, crying and whimpering that we will have to go there one by one. But our bloodshed should not remain unknown. A strong wind carried our cries deep into the night, as each one of us looks for a place to hide. We were told by people from nearby villages that when the murderers arrive, if we hide ourselves and they don't find us, it will be a lucky hour.

I had two little children, a little boy that was seven months old and the second child was two and a half years old. I wrapped them both on and around me and we hid in a potato cellar.

(My mother, again thinking that the microphone was off, says that my brother was only 7 months old. Actually, since this was now April 1942, my brother was 20 months old based on his birthday of August 17, 1940, and I was almost four years old, born on July 22, 1938. – H.M.)

The night passed as I sat with my two innocent children in the cellar. As it became four in the morning, I heard shooting and crying, but I sat there almost passed out with my children. I heard over my head in my house the murderers with heavy feet and big steps who were searching and yelling "rouse, rouse," get out, get out.

(A side comment from my mother: "This was the beginning of the first mass slaughter in our village that I write about." – H.M.)

We sat frightened and huddled together. My children sensed and understood the great danger around us. I soon felt that the first danger was over. It became quiet; there was no more shooting. My husband carefully opened the cellar door and let us out. He said the murderers have driven away and we could come out of the cellar. I entered my house very carefully and the spark of hope in my heart went out. A scream emerged from my throat that I am missing my near and dear ones, my mother and my brother.

My husband told me that there was a terrible tragedy. The Germans slaughtered 800 people, mostly children and the elderly. And what did I find when I left the cellar about my dear ones and my loved ones who sat the whole night in a hidden false wall? I knew about this wall. It was hardly wide enough to hold a sewing machine. I was told that my mother, my younger brother, my sister-in-law and their four children lay there the entire night, half alive, almost suffocating. They heard calls from the street in Russian that they need only to show their papers.

(Again, not knowing the microphone was still on, my mother said to me, "Do you know what was happening? My dear ones, my loved ones were lured out of their hiding places." – H.M.)

These were honest people with kosher and holy souls who were quickly taken by the waiting police who pointed their rifles at the backs of my dear relatives. They were taken away to their graves. My holy mother was 73 years old.

My brother and sister-in-law and their twenty year old daughter all became frantic as they were led to their deaths. Also Raiseleh, a seventeen year old daughter, Payke who was fourteen years old, and Henachke who was six years old, met the same fate. I will never forget that my beautiful and loving *mishpoche* (family) went to be slaughtered. I will always see you before my eyes and will never forget you. I see before me my family, their hands wrenched, as they take away my family. Children who were forcefully taken from their mother's arms became orphans in that one day.

(After the massacre, the remaining Jewish villagers went to view the grave site. – H.M.)

They walked that day with their faces wrapped in black. I was not able to recognize anyone. Some went quickly, and did not see everything. Others could not go. Some went slowly, barely with enough strength. But the screaming to the heavens was the same, "God why has this happened to us?" With a remembrance of their loved ones, their family, their relatives at the holy grave site, everyone was jealous of those who had perished.

(There was a feeling of jealousy of those who were murdered, since the surviving Jews wanted their lives to be ended so they

would no longer have to endure the torturous waiting for predictable fate that awaited them. My mother writes about this later on. – H.M.)

This is how our days appeared. Memorial lights burned in each household. From each household there was someone missing. And from every house you could hear hysterical outcries, as the last words of the holy victim were remembered. "Mother dear, where are we going?" "My dear child, where are they taking us?" Eight hundred hearts stopped beating.

(These were the words and questions asked by the innocent children who did not realize what fate awaited them; death from a German bullet. – H.M.)

◊ ◊ ◊

And now began more *tzsores* (troubles). Every day there are new edicts. We already knew what awaited us. We would receive news from neighboring villagers that the program was to make *"Jueden Rayn"* (clean out the Jews). Therefore we know our end. But how do we hold ourselves together? How can we survive this? This is all strange to us. We are jealous of those who are dead. The lucky person is the one who can do something, such as committing suicide. But what shall become of the children? What shall we do with the children? First do yourself in or first dispose of the children? The thought of that alone is a bitter one, and you can go crazy just thinking about it. Those were our bitter thoughts.

8

We did not sleep at night. Celebrations of any kind were not appropriate. Very few words were spoken with one another. We stopped crying. Our strength was gone. If you looked out the door or window, a peasant would point to the place where a chicken was being slaughtered. The peasant would show a cutting motion across his neck, saying that your good days are coming to an end, today or tomorrow.

◊ ◊ ◊

The dark day came. The nearby villagers had helped outfit the Germans with clean uniforms. The Germans made a circle with their trucks and took up their places. Our village was encircled. It was on August 6, 1942. The Germans and their accomplices surrounded the ghetto. Soon afterwards we heard cries and shooting.

I and my children ran into our hiding place in our backyard under the toilet, or *klozeh* as they called it in Zhetel. The waste pail stood on top of wooden planks. Underneath the planks was our hiding place, which was a small area dug out of the earth. Inside the hiding place was my mother-in-law, brother- and sister-in-law, their two children, my husband's sister, my mother-in-law's mother, my nephew, and two boys from the city of Luptz; thirteen people all crammed together. We sat there still like stones. We sat there numb and frightened; not a word was spoken. From the street we could hear screams and whimpering from women and children being led to their slaughter.

In our dug out hiding place, we could not tell the difference between day and night. But the shooting had quieted down, so we understood that it must be evening. From time to time we could hear the sounds of passing wagons and also the sounds of peasants who came to rob Jewish homes. We sat all night. Very early the next day we again heard shooting. That was most likely the Jews that were discovered in other hiding places, gathered up and led to the mass grave and shot.

Several such panicky days and nights passed in the same manner. We sat very close to each other in the hiding place. I sat in a suffocated, cramped, dirty place. The air inside became unbearable. My younger little boy was a little less than two years old and was already half dead. His clothing was rotted from the foul smell and dampness. My children survived on a lick of sugar that I remembered to bring with me into the hiding place.

The atmosphere in the cellar was punishing. The foul smell made us thirsty. Our lips were parched and split. With the urine water that my mother-in-law's mother gave, I was able to wipe my children's lips and that relieved their thirst for a few hours.

We were envious of those who had perished. They did not have to endure the terrible suffering and torture that we had yet to overcome. Can you image what it is like to be envious of those who already were dead and whose suffering is already over?

Three days and three nights stretched on as we sat in our hiding place. As time passed, we could no longer tolerate our terrible confinement. We felt that we were suffocating and, worst of all, we felt the danger to our little children as we see this before our eyes.

(My mother could hear the sounds resonating through the walls and into our hiding place. The sounds were coming from above the ground and she writes about what she heard. – H.M.)

The Germans had punished us a great deal. I will never forget the ongoing screaming and the whimpering from the Jewish children outside. "Mother, where are they taking us?" "My dear mother, who will hear our screams?" And as we lay in the hiding place, night came. We thought it was nighttime because the shooting had quieted down. But we were not able to stick our heads out because our peasant neighbors came into our house to rob our possessions and would surely give us away to the Germans. They arrived with horses and wagons in our yard. We heard them packing away into the wagons all our goods and possessions. But that did not bother us. The horrors of the preceding days made us immune.

In the morning we again hear shooting. The Germans had rounded up the Jews into the synagogue. From there the Germans would load their trucks with the Jews. As the trucks pulled away with its load of people, the people would yell and cheer, "Hurrah, our blood will be avenged."

Friends and dear ones told me that an appeal was made to the German officer in charge, the *Sondefüehrer* (a special German leader): "I am so young, I want to live." The Sondefüehrer just laughed and said sarcastically, "Ha, ha, she wants to live." The small request was drowned out quickly with rapid shots, from which the German guns were shooting twenty-five bullets every minute at the mass gravesite.

(Either my father or one of the gentiles must have told my mother about the rate of fire of twenty-five bullets every minute. My mother had no prior knowledge of weapons. – H.M.)

ON THE RUN TO THE FOREST

Three days and nights passed and we could no longer tolerate our terrible confinement in the hiding place.

(Based on my Cousin Kalman's autobiography, we were all in the hiding place from Thursday, August 6, 1942, until Saturday, about midnight, August 9, 1942. [2,3] – H.M.)

The next night when the hiding place was flooded with human waste, I decided that it would be better to perish from a German bullet rather than to suffocate from the foul air and the human waste. I took my little boy in my arms. He felt as if I was *schlepping* (carrying) a wet *onyetzeh* (rag). My second little boy, who was four year old, held on to my dress. It is difficult for me to write about my leaving the foul smelling hiding place. I decided to go to my mother's home and remain there until I am found by the Germans and shot. It appeared to me that this was to be my last wish. Each moment I asked for my death.

(My mother told me that when we all left the hiding place, a decision was made that we should all separate so we would have a better chance of survival. My mother, brother and I

*were in one group, and the others formed two more groups. –
H.M.)*

My mother-in-law and sister-in-law were with me when we
left our hiding place. They told me that they were not young
and maybe they would be able to get to some other place. I had
no idea in mind where to go once we left the hiding place.
When my mother-in-law left the hiding place she had lost her
eyesight. She could hardly walk and kept falling down. Her
daughter would not leave her side and so they both stopped
moving. Soon it became daylight and they were captured by
the Germans.

The Germans first took them to the other people that were
found. My mother-in-law and her daughter were lead to the
mass grave and they were all shot there. They had already
fought their battle. I was later told that my mother-in-law tried
to choke herself with the cherries that she received from the
peasants who took pity on the Jews.

This is difficult to write. I first felt that I should go to my
close family; namely to my mother's house and remain there,
where the Germans would kill me. It is as if they were asking
me what my last wish was before my death. And that was my
wish. And where was my mother?

*(My mother already knew that her mother, my grandmother,
was among the victims that had already perished. She asks
"And where was my mother?" rhetorically. – H.M.)*

At my mother's house, everything was already removed
and taken away. The only items remaining were a broken stove

13

that the wind was going through, as if to cry for each person, and some straw, a few bricks, broken dishes, broken glass, and some albums that contained memories about how I enjoyed my younger days. And now where do I take you, my dear ones?

I will be lucky to go where I have chosen. I am close to fulfilling my dreadful wish. A peasant that lived near my mother's house comes out. He was not a bad neighbor. But as soon as he saw me with my children laying on the ground, he grabbed a shovel and warns me that if I don't leave within five minutes, he will cut me and the children to pieces. Later he recognizes me and he tells me that his own family will be in danger if he allows me to remain lying there, since his home is nearby. The murderers have issued orders that if anyone hides a Jew, he and his family will be shot in the same manner as the Jews.

I told the peasant I could not run anymore and that for six days the children did not have any water to drink. He gave us some water.

The peasant became a little softer and offered us an alternative hiding place. Our home was in the ghetto. It was not far from the cemetery. So he advised us to go there because the graves from the dead were still open. The peasant tells me that the work at the gravesite was still going on, and although they find Jews in hiding there, the peasants cannot kill the Jews, so they leave the Jews at the gravesite.

(The ghetto area was not completely sealed off. Consequently one could sneak out in the dark of night. – H.M.)

The peasant tells me to hurry along. He doesn't have the heart to kill me, but he drives me to go quickly. I feel the blood dripping from my feet. It was from the broken glass on the street that I walked on during the night. It was quiet, but there were burned items, broken pieces of dishes, and shattered windows. I continued walking with my last blood and sweat towards the graves. I could hear the weak and feeble; moaning, gasping and rasping sounds of dying people. I heard the last guttural sounds of the dying.

I cannot find the words to explain or tell, but in my heart the memories will always remain there. It was dark – my older little boy understood everything. I was sure that I personally knew the half-dead people who were crying out and weeping. Forgive me, my loved ones, but I went by. I go and walk away with my eyes, my thoughts and my heart with all of you. But with my eyes, my feet, my children, and my instinct, I am driven forward to try and run; but to where I ask you?

◊ ◊ ◊

Daybreak began. From a distance I could see a house, so I walked over to it. A large dog came out to face me. The dog ripped off a piece of my old coat together with a piece of my flesh. Not far from the house, I fell by a nearby stream. Exhausted, I used my hands to scoop up some water for me and wetted my children's parched lips.

I gently shook my small little boy. He was dry and thin with sores and he appeared like a small piece of raw meat. And while I am lying down, I hear a policeman yelling as he was leaving a house that just this minute he saw a woman with two children. And the peasant starts running to look for us. I placed my face into the earth, and I and my children await our death, which is now nearer because we hear shooting. They are looking left and right and on all sides, but they don't see us. The policeman continued on his way. We lay in our place for an hour and I was sure that we were dead. I was not sure if I was shot or if I was alive. The bullets were whizzing by all around us, but we avoided them. It was one of my scariest moments.

Once again, I returned to the peasant where I wanted to find a way to die. However, the peasant brought out a piece of bread and tells me to go quickly. He was crying just looking at me and he doesn't have the heart to look at us any longer.

Now I walked the entire morning. I became confused and I went on bad paths and trails. The risk was unbearable. I placed my life in jeopardy. That very same morning I was going out of my mind. As I walked I avoided large roads until I entered a small forest. I fell onto the earth. I had the small piece of hard bread that I had received from the peasant. My children had not eaten for six days. With their little trembling hands, the children ate the bread and fell asleep. I sit on the ground and look up at the sky and talk to myself. What should I do with myself? Where shall I go? Why should I be suffering so long? Wouldn't it be better if I had perished with the others?

I hear shepherds coming. They are laughing loudly. They are glad to see me and ask if I have any money. They are young gentile boys, but they know everything about taking and stealing money. They must know that I don't have much, not even our souls. They took from me a few rubles and a few other things that I had with me. They could make very little from these things they took.

I soon left this place through the fields and woods. It came to my mind that I should go to a peasant lady that I knew very well and was a good friend before the war. Maybe I could leave one of my children or both children with her; perhaps my children will survive there. I remind myself that she was a very good Christian woman, with a good heart. She attended church. I will go through the woods. And as soon as it gets dark, I will enter her home because then no one will see me. Then maybe I can stay with her and sleep and perhaps have one good meal before I die.

I cannot stand on my feet. Now I have a fresh thought. I walk over to her house and she sees me; she cries and crosses herself. She gives me a shirt to wrap over the children and a coat for me. She lets me go on top to her attic and tells me that it has become quiet for now and also tells me the news as to what is going on around us in our town, how the chaos appears. She has a good heart. She could not bear to watch how the Germans led the tortured, half-conscious Jews. She is very nice and she gives me some soup with milk, which I shall not quickly forget. We had not eaten for a long time. I was getting sleepy and fell asleep. During all this time I did not close my eyes to get any sound sleep. The children fell asleep.

(My mother was so physically and mentally exhausted that she could only sleep in small intervals, always on guard and fearful of being discovered by the Germans – H.M.)

It probably did not take long when I feel someone pulling at my feet. The peasant woman is holding a pitchfork and yelling at me that I must leave immediately because she heard that people pay with their lives for hiding Jews. She does not want to hear any excuses: she does not want to lose a minute. She is holding the pitchfork in her hands and says that I must leave right now. I cry and pull my hair from my head and plead with her to let us remain and sleep just one night. I ask her to look at the wounds on my feet and upon my children. She takes pity on us and comes up with a plan. As it is now midnight, she will help me and will carry one child for about seven or eight miles away to where two nuns live. She tells me that I and my children should lie by the nuns' window. When the nuns get up in the morning to pray, they will see me. And since the nuns are not allowed to tolerate the sight of blood, they will perhaps do something for me.

(The reference to "blood" was probably a superstition among the peasants since there are no facts available to substantiate this premise. – H.M.)

Suddenly, the peasant lady immediately grabs and pulls me by my hair and I fall down from the attic. Her son grabs my older son and drags him through the corn, which was fairly high and as I write this before my eyes, I see him dragging my older son by his neck, a half-alive child. I carry in my arms my other weak little child who is a *shvacher neffeshly* (weak soul). We go on. It hardly feels that I am on my two feet, but rather as if I was walking on sticks.

Unexpectedly, the peasant lady's son, who has been our guide, abandons us. He turned back and left us alone. It began to rain. We lay in the rain. We are wet and cold and I hear coughing from my little child. I am frightened because now we can be heard from our hiding place. The darkness begins to turn into daybreak. I see the two old nuns arise from their places and begin their daily prayers. The nuns see me and the children. After their prayers, they open their door and take us inside. The large crosses on their hearts are in front of our eyes; the crosses are hanging from their necks. They approach us slowly and make the sign of the cross.

The house is hot and full of flies; I understand that they never bothered to even kill a fly on the wall. When they saw us they became frightened and gave my children milk and soon gave us an *ehtizhe* (a plan, or a solution). The day before, the police and the Germans found many Jews that were in hiding. They don't want to betray us to the police or to the Germans and instead tell me that they will lead us to a place near the *shtetl* (town) where there is some hay and where I can rest my feet a bit. They wrapped my feet in linen bandages, because my feet were swollen from all the walking. They tell me not to think about my hunger, but they help me find something to eat. The piece of bread from the night before still lingers in my throat.

At two o'clock in the morning, one of the nuns comes to tell me that the police are searching every stall and barn and that I am in great danger. As I understand the meaning, I feel my blood rising. The nun takes me by the hand and with my barefoot son, leads us into a cornfield that was not yet cut down. I laid down on the ground and now I began to feel the pain. My little son was making sounds like a little bird. I could not understand him. His face was covered with large sores caused by the dirt. He did not look like a child, but more like a *bah-shefenesh* (a sub-human creature). I let him lay; he could not cry; he was very weak and did not have any strength. For three days and three nights I hid in the cornfield until the time came for the corn to be cut down. They chased me away then.

Then it was my end. The nuns gave me enough food to eat. But I had to keep going on. To where? I began again to wander. I went for two miles and there was a lake. I thought this was where I can drown myself together with my children. My God, give me the strength to go together with both my children into the water.

◊ ◊ ◊

I still cannot understand how by my own hands that I can leave my child. I leave my small boy alone and I walk away a half mile and he does not cry. I am sure that my child understood me when I left him. But more than a half a mile I could not go. My child's eyes begged me, don't leave me mother. Let us stay together mother. And so I turned back and I saw a peasant looking at me through the windows.

I later heard from a peasant that I looked like a crazy person, with both children in my arms. From time to time I would lay both children down and would lie down myself. Then I would leave both children and walk alone for a while, only to return to take them both back with me. To the peasants, it appeared their Jesus has stopped me from abandoning my children. Just minutes before, there were murderers on that same path that I had just walked.

I arrived at a place where a peasant wanted to take me back to the village where he said he could obtain some money for turning me in. And this was for certain, a sure thing.

(This was the 600 Mark reward that the Germans paid for each Jew that was caught and brought to them. – H.M.)

But then he changed his mind. It appeared to be too far for him to take us back into the village. He then gave me a warning. If, in the next five minutes I ran into the woods so that he would not see me, then I could save my life. He appeared big and wild with a scythe in his hand. He shows me that a scythe can cut a neck very good. Then I thought and asked myself, how can I run with my two small children? But I ran into the woods and then he left me alone.

◊ ◊ ◊

Now I find myself in a small forest. I hear talking. Someone is coming and talking. And to our luck it is a much nicer peasant lady. She saw me and my children and began to cry. She tells me that she cannot tolerate our situation. She will give us food to eat. Her house is not far away. But I have fear and compassion for her. There are neighbors close by her house. I fear that those neighbors would come and report us to the Germans. This lady is taking a big risk to help us. We ate as much as we wanted. But it is difficult to eat too much because we have been hungry for so many days.

For half a day and the night, I remained not far from the place where I laid the night before. I did not feel cold or warm. I had not slept for several days, so the ground beneath me felt soft and everything around me felt good. My nature was much better than my person. When a person's nature becomes bad, it is like a storm. But a storm only last for a while, perhaps an hour. How long will my personal storm last? Oh, how good the night is. Who knows what tomorrow will bring? It is a big question for each of us. The sky is dark. I must feel around in the dark, but I am still alive and things are good.

It becomes daylight. With great fright I get up. I see before my eyes two boney little souls. The little eyes open and ask for food and drink. The children ask, mother will we live? Is it possible? But I know my answer in my heart that it would be impossible with two children. I did not hurry. Where do I go? The moment arrives when I decide to go where my eyes will lead me, or as it is said, I will go where my eyes will carry me.

Barefooted, I go deeper into the woods. I again went to a peasant and his wife that I had seen with children around their house. They saw me and clasped their hands like the rest. This was a better peasant. The peasant gave me a potato and something to eat. The peasant tells me that it does not matter if I go to sleep, as if to tell me that I will not survive anyway. He tells me of the many Jews that he saw running into the woods, young girls alone, all running away from the massacre. The peasant says he also saw men with rifles – partisans. He advises me that I should try to go further into the woods where they all are going. It is there where the few Jews are. He says that eventually there won't be any survivors. But he tells me to go, don't remain near here.

The peasant shows me the direction where to go and I again walked for six miles. It took all my strength. I was going on nervous energy. One child in my arms and one child by the hand. Both children were unnatural looking, *ibergekerte* (turned upside down) and dark like dirt. I decided on a certain spot and there I again bedded down for the night. I feel the cold; it is wet. The woods are wet. From time to time the trees are breaking; later on I hear the forest mice and the snakes slide by my ears. But who cares? It means nothing. This time the night did not go by so quickly. It is hard to sleep and there is no sign of hope. I don't have any hope. How long can I hold out?

I have a thought. I will go to a peasant who knew me before the war began. The peasant was good to the Jews. And I will tell him everything because he was a friend of the Jews. Because this is what I still remember, what he said before the war. He lives deep in the woods, far from the village. Maybe he will have pity on us.

I started to walk once more. I am on the road for six days and six nights now. And what will happen, where is my home and where will I arrive? My spirit rose and I went ten miles. I spoke to my older son. Come, let's go my dear son. My son tried to walk quickly when we had to go through a dangerous area. As we went through dangerous areas, my children shivered as though they knew fear.

I don't understand with what strength I had to go so many miles during the six days. If I went on a straight path, I would not have to walk so far. But during the previous days I was going, I was all mixed up and confused and I went around in circles. And now I am going to the peasant that I remember, the one that lives deep in the Pushner woods. It was in the evening when he saw me and he turns his back like he does not know me.

I begin to call to him by name, Verabeh, to cry, to beg him, but it does not help. I lay down a little bit further from his house, because he chased me away. I became crazed and began beating my fists on my children's backs, wanting to kill them. But that sight the peasant could not bear to see. And neither could his wife and his two small daughters. They began to cry and begged their father that he should let us stay overnight in the place where they keep their pigs. But he did not want us to stay.

There was a cold wind; my feet were all beaten up. The skins on the faces of my children were full of blisters. Because of the dirt on their faces, you could only see their little eyes. The scene of both the peasant's and my hysterical family caused the peasant's heart to soften and he allowed me to lie down to sleep in a dugout area that I remember was for potatoes. The hole was deep and lined with straw so the potatoes should not freeze.

The dugout was far from the peasant's house on top of a small hill. The peasant led me to it and told me to go in. It was very deep and we needed a ladder. But I already dropped myself in. At the bottom there were several rotting potatoes. In the springtime the peasants remove the good potatoes and leave the bad ones in the hole. I gathered some dirty straw that was lying about; it was soft and I placed it under my feet. The pit was full of frogs. After me, the peasant threw in my children. Then I looked up with my eyes to the sky to see where I was. I was deep in the earth.

When the peasant left us, I thought of the devil coming and a great fear overwhelmed me. I thought that at any minute the peasant would come with a shovel and pour dirt into the hole. It would be very simple for the peasant, since he would not need to explain anything to anyone. And if the peasant wants to be a patriotic person, he can obtain 600 Marks for our three souls – the reward that the Germans paid for Jews. I ask you my dear people, how large was my hope and who was watching out for us and who knew what will be? I knew my situation very well. I will also well-remember that night.

I began to throw out excess things from the hole, but it was impossible. The hole was too deep and as I threw out things, I would get the things back into my eyes. I could not make it easier for myself. My heart was heavy. And what am I now? I'm not a person and not an animal. God in Heaven, what should I do? In such circumstances, in such times neither death nor life comes. We remain in the world. My dear ones, you are better off. You already lie in peace. I am jealous of you and yet I miss you. You must understand how bitter it is to be jealous of those who are dead.

REUNITED WITH MY HUSBAND

My children fell asleep. I am on my knees and I hear shots over my head. All of a sudden I hear something coming. It must be an animal that passed by. It is once again quiet. I think that I hear things, but it must be my nerves and my imagination. That is the way it was all night until my weariness and my weakness took over. I fell inside the dugout hole and fell asleep for a short while. From the sky above, the color appeared light grey and I understood that daybreak was coming. My sleep did not last long. I jump up and see my husband standing over the potato hole. My husband is crying. I never in my life saw a man crying like that. He held in his hand half a *goiyishe* (gentile) *latke* (pancake) to give me and my children.

My husband ironically also escaped from the massacre into the woods. That is how he saved himself. As he was escaping and running into the woods, a pair of peasants told him that they saw his wife and both his children. He did not believe them. But some of our acquaintances told him and showed him where to go. So that is how he found us.

My husband stood over the hole, crying for about half an hour. We asked each other where shall we go now, and what shall we do with the children? We have to fight back, shoot, kill and burn. We can all perish doing that. You cannot leave anything that will lead back to yourself. Our close friends have sought revenge. I can hear them calling today. But what shall we do with the children?

My husband took off a pair of torn sandals and gave them to me. He said that if it were not for the children, we would go right into battle. But for now he asks me to stay around here. He knows a few more people that have escaped into the woods. He will take me to them. But everything would be much better without children. With children, no one wants to be associated with you. Those who are already in the woods don't have their children. They know that with children it would be impossible to survive.

But what shall we do now? Where can I hide myself? I climbed out of the hole with my last strength and went over to a place where there was a wooden lean-to platform. That is where the peasants stored their hay. They would take the hay from wet areas where a horse and wagon could not pass.

◊ ◊ ◊

We are now in the woods for three months. There I already met about ten people. Among them is a pair of orphans, a pair of young women. The mood is very sad. We don't speak to each other. We don't ask each other any questions, nor do we engage in any idle talk. No one wants to sit close to me because I am with two children. If a child begins to cry, it could bring upon us a terrible catastrophe. And everyone wants to remain alive not just to live, but to take *nekomeh* (revenge).

From my husband I find out that that the partisans are gathering themselves to prepare for a mission to fight and to kill the Germans. My husband cannot remain with me in the civilian camp for women and children. Such camps can be easily located by locals anxious to collect the rewards offered by the Germans. And besides that, my husband volunteered for this mission because he did not know that I and his children were alive. Consequently, my husband was immediately enlisted into the group that was going into battle. He leaves to join up with the other partisans and I remain in the civilian camp in the forest. And I know there is nothing that I do or can say.

◊ ◊ ◊

Little by little, people abandon me. My little boy began to suffer sores from the mosquitoes. The mosquitoes ate at his blisters and he cried. Anyone who had a ready hand hit him, cutting his skin. Believe me that this still remains a vision in my eyes how it looked.

Now we were becoming accustomed to these woods. We already had slept in the woods for several nights. We received food from a Christian partisan who is passing through. When he saw me he told me that I reminded him very much of his own family. He told me if I stayed at the same place, he would bring me bread a second time.

LIFE IN THE FOREST

And now we began our life in the woods. Days become short, nights become long. It becomes cold. What do we do with the children? They are barefooted. We walk over to a small stream. My children stand there. From afar come some shepherd children who run over to us. The shepherd children say, "Your children will soon freeze," and begin to laugh. My children ask, "Mother, what did they say?"

A hard winter is coming upon us. What can we think of to do next? My husband would come to us from time to time and bring something to eat – bread, sometimes meat. He would tell me what was going on and what the partisans were doing – sad, very sad stories with little hope of surviving. We received word that the Germans were spreading out all over. Also passing by our area were Russian partisans who were not in the mood to speak.

It was very bitter. Anyone who had an old rag or a *peltz* (a fur or a pelt, used to line a winter coat) carried it so as to have a place to lie down. We dug into the earth with our bare hands to make a sleeping area. We would bury ourselves deep into the ground. And a little later in the autumn, we already had dug ourselves deep into the earth. At night, even though it was very dangerous, we would go out and obtain some potatoes and dried peas. We stored them near our sleeping places. You can eat a whole day on a few of the dried peas. It is very *zetik* (nourishing), as they say in the old country.

At the beginning, the peasants would respond to us a little better, meaning they would give us a few things. But that also changed. They were taken advantage of. Everybody wanted to take from the peasants. They complained that they didn't have enough to eat themselves. They could not go to too many places. Most places were occupied by the Germans. So obviously, we could not go there either. So you can understand that the situation was becoming worse and worse. Our food supply was just enough to get by on.

There are stories and rumors running among the peasants that at the front the Germans were getting hit hard in their backs. We understand that our situation is getting better at our small front. We live day by day with hope.

◊ ◊ ◊

My little son has begun to walk around in the woods, but without shoes. The frost is very cold. His tiny feet are red. He walks and he runs, but his feet are freezing. I prepare a small fire so he can warm his little feet. I have a discussion with my older boy about everything. He is three and a half years old. He already knows that we have to be very quiet so no one would hear us, and also that we should not make the fire any bigger. He understood very well the danger of being seen if the fire is too large. We rely on the fire for food. Once the embers are sufficiently hot, we can bake some potatoes and some beans.

Our safest times are during the night. It was during the nice times during the day, when various catastrophes can befall us. But at night, the forest is dark and obscure, so we are certain that we will survive the night.

From time to time we see a partisan pass by. We ask him what news he has. He tells us of various actions that have happened. He says that it is very dangerous for us to be where we are. This is because the peasants that are close by are motivated by the Germans to give us up, that is to inform the Germans where the Jews are hiding in the forest.

We have to be very careful. There should be no fires during the day. And above all my situation is hopeless because with two children it makes it impossible to avoid being captured by the enemy. My children overhear such talk. My heart becomes heavy with worry. I am left alone and I don't know what to do. I am worse than someone who has lice. People shy away from me slowly; they don't tell me when or why they go. My children always looked pitiful, and for pity would be the reason anyone would kill them.

◊ ◊ ◊

After a while, a few good months pass. By some miracle, it is just a miracle, we can go to sleep and are able to remain asleep. There is no lack of firewood in the forest. If your back is cold, then you turn over with your back towards the fire. If a piece of the blanket is burned then it just becomes a smaller blanket. But as a result we feel closer to the warmth of the fire. A short time later I met partisans who were wearing boots half burned by the fire (the result of sleeping too close to the fire).

A hard winter had begun. The fire helps us a great deal. I have been separated from everyone; everyone has abandoned me. My children were barefooted and without warm clothing. There was also no food for them. The situation is made worse because I don't have a shelter or place to go to. The enemy is chasing and harassing me. I feel that I am doomed. My fate is sealed; I won't need anything, because the inevitable will happen. But if I am secured with a place under the free sky, and there is mud and swamps, which makes the access to our place very difficult, in my eyes it appears and means that I have a home. I feel secure as we lay on our frozen ground. It is hard for me to believe my own words.

I have a sudden thought that I will go to one of the nearby peasants and ask for some milk. I will tell him that a miracle happened to me, or that I was lucky. Maybe I don't want to blurt out that I must feed my small children. I will ask him for little bit of food and maybe a pencil and a piece of paper. I want to write a letter to our small *shtetl*. There are many Gentile partisans here whose elderly mothers and fathers are in the village. Sometimes the partisans need things from their elders. They visit their elders, since being a Christian poses very little risk; they are allowed to go almost everywhere.

I decided to write a few words to a close lady friend of mine, a Polish pharmacist, who was very nice to me prior to the war. She is a very good natured woman. Even when we were in the ghetto, she would bring me many things to eat. That was a risk for her, but she did it anyway.

I went that night to the nearby peasant as I planned. I left my two children and I told them that I am going while it is quiet and because we don't hear any shooting. I want to try my luck. And as it became a little dark, I started my journey. I arrived at the nearby peasant's house and knocked on the door. I tell the peasant that my children have not had any milk for a long time and ask for anything that he can spare for my children and me. As for me, maybe he has an old kerchief he can spare. The peasant listened to me and then tells me that he doesn't like the Germans and that he helps the people in the woods; and above all he helps the partisans who fight against the Germans.

The peasant doesn't hesitate too much, and gives me a small pail with milk and some other things that I asked for. He even asks me to return tomorrow for more milk. Can you image what a good night I had? The peasant speaks with an open heart and tells me that the signs are that the Germans will lose the war. But the big question is whether we will survive until that time.

Now I go back to my little children. I leave the peasant's house; it is very dark and I can't see my hands in front of me. God in Heaven, how can I find the place where my children are? What kind of miracle can I hope for now? It does not help. As I go through the woods, the thorns on the branches tear at my skin. My small amount of milk fills up will pine needles, leaves and tree bark. I stopped on my way because I don't know where the children are. I cannot yell for my children; I would not dare make a sound. I feel that I have gone long enough to be at the right place. What should I do? Finally I yell out, "Children, where are you?" I don't receive an answer. The forest is quiet. I will wait until daylight when there is more light. But these are long winter nights.

I cry out "Henikel" to my older child. "My dear son, Henikel." I hear a small voice answer me. "Mother, Mother, here we are." We cannot talk too much for fear of being discovered. For a half hour I stood, walked and circled around trying to find my children. In my frustration, the milk spilled. I was left with no milk for the children. My feet ached and I fell on the ground. We will surely freeze and die of hunger.

A DESPERATE PLEA FOR FOOD

And now I write a letter to my Polish pharmacist friend. I can write Polish very well. I wrote the letter on a Sunday morning because I knew that she was a good woman, very religious and she would go to church every Sunday. My letter to her was with these words:

My dear woman, (with her name written in the greeting)
I know it is Sunday and that you are now in church. You are asking God that your children's house and your children's food supplies should not be confiscated.
God has given everyone the right to live and to be free. I am writing you these few words as my last hope. I find myself under the free sky and one God must take pity on me. My eyes

are full of tears and thus I cannot clearly see what I am writing to you. You don't need my speeches. I leave it for you to understand for yourself.

I gave this letter to a Christian partisan. Everyone knew about the pharmacy in the village, so the lady received the letter right away. It did not take long, no more than three days until I received a very nice package from her. There were all sorts of goods, even dried *farfehl* (small pellet-shaped noodles), potatoes, and flour. It was a gift from God. Even a single glove and a coat. Can you imagine my joy and what a holiday it was for us?

THE EARTH TREMBLES

I am still in the forest. But things cannot be good being in the forest. Any minute can be catastrophic. Right away, the same evening, shots can be heard. The earth trembles underneath us; we are used to hearing those sounds. Our partisans would test their rifles if the area was quiet. But the shooting sounds were now from an army with artillery and we are warned that many Germans and White Russian police are now coming.

(It was known that the White Russian police collaborated with the Germans against the Jewish partisans. – H.M.)

They are going to search the woods and trap us. That means there will be an *ablave* (a very thorough search) of the woods designed to trap us.

Before the Germans and White Russian police enter into the woods, they shoot into the woods. They use rockets and searchlights. Our teeth chatter. Where shall we bury ourselves? We hear various sounds from groups that run by with their rifles extended and who will stand up against the regular German army. Even family groups run and some stop by me, clasp their hands and say that God should only help you. They know very well that running in the woods with two children is impossible. Even walking is difficult, for there is snow and ice.

It now becomes a little lighter; it is daybreak. This is the second day of the search in the woods. The storm over the forest is terrible. Airplanes are overhead. Things are burning. From time to time I hear yelling and shooting. I take both my little children. Not a word is spoken, like they were deaf and dumb, and we move to another place about a half a mile away. The snow is deep. We make a path that is visible. This is not good. Above all it eats at my heart for my little children. I tuck my little child's feet into my naked bosom wanting to keep his feet warm, so his feet won't become frozen. I sit upon a felled tree and my children lay with their feet towards me and I keep them warm with my warm breathe the whole day.

Daytime events could at any moment become unpredictable. The roar of the heavy artillery was indescribable and something that you could not write about. I still don't understand how they searched the forest and that I and my children who are sitting so close to the enemy were not seen. That day we did not want to, and could not, eat.

It became nighttime. The sky was red from the fired shots that reached up into the sky. Our murderers were so very close. They burned down all the nearby houses where we would at times receive some food. The peasants that lived close to the forest were killed and their homes burned down. I saw sky and the forest in red, everything was burning. It is hard for me to sit in one place.

It becomes quieter. It appears that the Germans did not want any more shooting. It is very still. The smell of the burned cows and their meat has approached us. In the darkness we can hear people speaking.

NO FOOD, NO LIFE

With the night we become a little more secure. I hoped to go to my former place where I left some of my food and to see what was left of my supplies, but everything was gone. I find out that hungry partisans took everything and enjoyed themselves. I stand there with my hands wringed and clasped. Now I know for sure of my death. No food, no life.

My heart troubles me, not for me, I can bear the hunger, but surely for my children. Maybe some peas or some raw beets to eat? But those who pass by are also very hungry. What shall we do now, this night? What kind of a day will it be tomorrow? We don't know. For us the day is not good; after each night, the day comes. But your natural instinct tells you that today you must leave the place where you are.

◊ ◊ ◊

Another storm, other fires, and again we hear the cries of a peasant, "Jesus," as the peasant is shot. The forest was in chaos for two days. On the third day it is quieter. We are told that many people were burned on the road and that the Gentiles left when the fires broke out. We are left exposed to hunger. What shall we do now? Where do we go to find a little bit of food?

Time goes by and has its effect, and now I want something to eat. I will tell you the truth. I am not hungry, but I want something for the children. In the meantime some partisans pass by. They wonder how I and the children survived after such a search of the forest by the Germans. I don't know what to tell the partisans; because I really didn't understand the danger we were in. But what danger we were in has already happened and has passed. I tell the partisans that I can overcome hunger, but maybe they can see that the children should not die of starvation.

A partisan tells me that he doesn't know where there is any food. However, he told me that maybe there will be some food a few days later. Then he tells me that the murdered peasants had left potatoes in dugout holes and that I should go and get the potatoes because there were no people that remained. But it still would be dangerous and very difficult to hide. He had heard the Germans in the area. That night we had to take the risk. I and two other women and a man tell me that they are all very hungry and it will be difficult for them to hold out.

We set out the same night. We walked very slowly. It was about two miles from our original place. The snow was heavy and we had torn shoes. Our sweat and determination kept us warm. Now we arrive at our destination, at the dugout hole covered with deep snow near a burned out house. The only things standing are bare irons that initially scared us but act as guides. Now the question is where do we go from here to extract a few potatoes?

With a common understanding, we all fell down onto the earth and with our hands and nails clawed at the frozen ground. We felt for potatoes as if they were diamonds. The smell of the potatoes, as many as we had, satisfied my hunger right away.

By finding the potatoes we didn't have to worry anymore. There was now something to eat. I am ashamed to tell you that I took too many potatoes. That was because my eyes were bigger than my ability to carry so many potatoes. With such a load of potatoes, I fell and could not get up off the ground. I lost my strength and my will to keep going. I had a large unwieldy rag filled with potatoes and the weight of the potatoes caused me to lose my balance and fall upon the potatoes – and there I lay. My friends, the two women and the man, passed by and yelled at me that I wanted to take in the whole world. But I see before my eyes that they are going on with larger sacks of potatoes and even more in their pockets and in their hats. I have much less than they do, but yet they make fun of me. At that point my strength left me, together with my will. I now realized that I had taken more of a load of potatoes than I could carry.

With newfound strength, I took some more potatoes. Everything seems to repeat itself. I stand up on my feet and I begin to walk but I can't. My partners are far from me. I leave half the load and run. I arrive at my little children. They already smell the potatoes; they feel the satisfaction that they will have some food. That same night we had baked potatoes. But when I ate them they were still hard and without salt, so I threw up.

HOW LONG CAN THIS LAST?

The next morning it was quiet as if after a fire. Partisans pass by and tell me that they lost many people in the forest who had weapons, meaning other partisans. Women and children perished, which means that our situation had become worse. If the Germans were able the first time to be aggressive and wipe out about forty percent of the people in the forest, we are certain that they will soon return for the remaining partisans.

We were warned about the suffering that the Germans created for the Jews that ran. The Germans caught them alive. We were *nakeim* (sorry) for those that were caught alive because those people were tortured. Even if they caught small children, boys and girls, they would be tortured like the partisans. The Germans also caught Jews who became lost. Those Jews were killed ruthlessly. They were given a terrible death by the Germans. Our hopes are that a humane and quick death awaits us.

◊ ◊ ◊

Days go by. We hear sad news that this person has fallen in battle under such and such circumstances; another has died under different conditions. We forget about everyday aspects of living such as tables, benches and beds. And I am ashamed to say that we forget about all those friend and relatives that we abandoned who may still be alive. Where are they? Were they caught? Maybe some of the people we knew are still alive. We see day by day that there are less people.

We hear news and sometimes rumors. Some people were just caught. And another person was taken away. There are those that perished from frostbitten feet. A mother told me that her daughter, just eight years old, lost her feet the other night during the shooting. The mother held her daughter but her small feet were just hanging and her daughter did not feel her tiny feet anymore from the cold. And so this was the way it was each night as we sat by the fire.

A few people approach me, but rarely do they tell me about the various sad occurrences, but they always tell me that God should only help me with my two small children, just to make small talk. "How are you surviving, and what do you think?" How should I answer them? Is this a situation where I am violating a law? Can I make everything well again? From time to time we receive more food.

◊ ◊ ◊

My husband would arrive at our civilian camp, barely escaping death. He would travel many miles on the run because he and the other partisans were being chased. Partisans were like fugitives, always being searched for. It was good to see my husband, but how long can this last? We make fires to keep warm.

SEASONS IN THE FOREST

Spring is beginning. The earth is now opening up. The snow is melting and exposing the ground underneath the snow. There is a lot of water. You can now see the wildness of the forest: overturned trees, trees with holes from the winter homes of mice nests. Then the large mice came out, looked at us as if to say, "Why do we need these humans in our forest?" My children saw this like it was something natural. My children were growing up together with the mice. They think that this is the way things should be. The mice have the right to live, but not us.

My children play with the trees and so do the mice. It was all very natural. The mice would wait until the little nuts dropped down from the trees. My small boys would also wait for the nuts to drop down. They would gather and hide them for later on because it was bitter times. However, the mice were very smart and found my children's hiding place and took away the nuts. My children could not understand who was taking away their hidden nuts. We get used the living in the forest.

◊ ◊ ◊

Summer comes and brings food stuffs. Blueberries – red ones, black ones – sweet sap from the trees. It is such a *mechaye* (pleasure) that my mouth is watering from the blueberries. With the blueberries, I want a piece of bread.

Things are a little better, but we are still hungry. We are looking for food like animals. Various grasses begin to sprout.

We try to cook a variety of plants to eat. We have forgotten about the world, about the good times, *haminke chalochim* (dreams about our home), when we had a bed to sleep in. I know and still feel this as if it was a dream.

And now I have the instinct of an animal with the face of a human being. You would not believe what we are becoming and getting used to. You must understand that the forest had overtaken us with its dirt. Our faces were always dark from the black burned wood embers, which were like coal or coal dust, black and filthy. We did not have any matches. And if we did manage to have some matches, they were never dry. What do we do to keep the matches dry if we don't have a roof over our heads? The best we could do to keep the fire burning was with hot coals from ongoing fires. If I did not see any danger before me, we made a fire from day to night with those coals whenever it was possible.

◊ ◊ ◊

The Germans were all around us. And so the summer passed with various catastrophes such as trying to find and bring back food. People were caught alive. Each step was dangerous; your life was always at stake.

My husband tries to come to see me whenever it is possible. If it is quiet around the area, he brings us bread and even some meat. The place where he is camped with the fighting partisans is at great risk of being discovered. There are always hardships to obtain any food. We are almost in the hands of the murderers. Most of our people who were originally in the forest with us have already perished.

◊ ◊ ◊

The harsh winter is again upon us. With what can we do to prepare ourselves? We agree that the best thing to do is not to stay in one place. The peasants already know that we are here and they can bring the Germans. The best solution is for everyone to go to a new place, about five miles further away.

We gather up all that we have and go for miles. My husband was with us and he helped me relocate. My children are already walking on their own; I don't have to carry them in my arms. A few other people came along with us. Since the new place is deep in the forest, we know it will be difficult to find the place again. It will be hard for anyone to chase us out.

So what do we do to find the new hiding place? We decide to bark like a dog to signal our friends when we approach the hiding place. In return, those in the hiding place will answer like a barking dog to signal that it is safe; it was like a password. The hiding place was not far from a village that the partisans pass by.

We slept there that night. It was very wet. I don't know if that place had ever had human footsteps there. It was a swamp. But that did not mean anything. We sit in a group of six people and we listen and hear the twigs snapping; my God who can it be? One of the men ventures out and sees a peasant gathering a certain type of tree to make wheels. The trees were especially good for that purpose because the wood became hard during autumn. The peasant saw us, became scared and began to run. We could no longer remain there. It was too dangerous. The peasant would bring the Germans or police back with him. There were too few of us to chase after him.

We became very scared. What do we do now? Where shall we go now? I am now the *kapore hindele* (sacrificial chicken), and left alone. I am the worse one to go with. They all left me and I am alone like a person who is the odd one, a leftover in God's world, one who does not belong because I have my children with me, who can accidently give away our hiding place.

I sit again under the free sky and I again decide that I must not go anywhere. If I go for any food, I will be exposed right away and put to death. And those that did expose themselves to get food did not do any better. If it is *bashert* (so willed), I will remain alive another day, maybe another week, and another month. What more can I hope for? What is awaiting me?

I wandered over to another place, very close by. There I decided to remain alone. Another woman comes over to me. Her name is Rodiya. She is also alone with two daughters. It is not a good situation, not what I wanted; no men and no rifles. She also could not find a place and she was also not wanted because she had two children and no weapons.

◊ ◊ ◊

Another autumn rain begins, with broad white feather-looking snow. The rain and snow soaked our bodies. We can no longer sit there; our clothing is soaked and all wet; we feel the extra weight on our shoulders. The rain and snow continue and it covers the earth and trees with whiteness. The wind sends a chill through our bones.

I want to cover my arms but I can't because cold water is dripping from me and the sides of my clothing are already freezing. A fright came over me that I will freeze to death. In desperation, I began to cry. My children looked at me and began to cry. The crying did not help but it made it a little easier on my heart. And as we were crying, my husband showed up. He immediately constructed a small lean-to with a roof from sticks right on our spot to provide us some shelter. I crawled inside and that became our home.

◊ ◊ ◊

Winter is pushing its way in and now we must dig again into the earth with shovels that we found on peasants' graves. We used some tools that were in the forest. Everything was the ultimate responsibility of the men, even in the forest, to prepare hiding places for the winter, before the snow hides everything. The women and children worked alongside the men.

We tried to be very clever and sharpen our wits to deceive our enemies. We build several hiding places that could be accessed from the *zemlyanka* (a camouflaged hiding place). We make tunnels underneath our *zemlyanka*. If someone were to pass by, they would only see the crude lean-to shelters. We made the tunnel entrances so it would appear that they were wells or holes filled with water. We also made hiding places underneath fallen trees. The entrances to these hiding places were cleverly camouflaged.

That winter we learned how to live, hide and survive in the forest, how to make corn flour, find peas, and use hay and straw. The little bit of flour kept us alive. In the dugout hole it was very dirty. The corn was not milled properly because the Germans had burned down all the mills. It was very dangerous to go to a mill close to the village. Nevertheless, from our unmilled corn we could survive and not die of hunger.

A lady and a young woman join us. From time to time we receive some food stuff from the partisans who pass by. We usually go to the area that we expect the partisans to pass through. Two young boys that escaped, about fourteen years of age, have joined up near us. They go out to gather firewood.

◊ ◊ ◊

The Germans are occupied fighting on the front during the winter months. It appears that the Germans have forgotten about the Jews. We hear news from the peasants. They tell us that the Germans are planning a very large *ablaveh* (search and trap operation) of the forest. We know that when the peasants start to speak, that they must know something. We all become saddened, and we take stock of how many of us are left. What kind of hope can we now have? All of a sudden we felt that everything was burning all around us.

The Russian non-Jewish partisans place all the blame on the Jews. They also say that the Jews are wandering around the homes begging for bread. They say that Jews are helping the Germans by making arms. There were reports of forced labor camps where Jews were making war material for the Germans. The Russian partisans also say that the Jews are spies.

It is the beginning of a large anti-Semitic sentiment in the forest. Young Jewish boys are being shot for begging for bread. A Jewish man and woman were beheaded with an axe by anti-Semitic *goieshe* (gentile) bandits. These bandits were a known group of partisans that were not aligned with the Germans. The biggest problem is that we cannot go out a few steps. The forest has become too dangerous, even from our own brothers that live with us in the forest. But we can still hide ourselves with some hope.

THE FOREST IS SURROUNDED BY GERMANS

More sad news. People get drunk and shoot one another. There is no right and no wrong.

Winter goes by and spring is approaching. Water seeps into our dugout holes in the ground. We become soaked. We use sticks to try to lay above the water. But we cannot think about that. A strong force is approaching us in the forest - about 40,000 Germans, a regular army. We are surrounded on all sides and we don't know what to do.

The Germans want to make sure that no one will be left alive this time because the Germans want to enter the forest with great force. They even announce it in the newspapers that they are preparing attacks on the White Russian forests. They want to burn and destroy each and every partisan and anything else that is hidden in the woods.

We hear the airplanes low overhead. They are coming at us with the latest weapons, artillery, rockets, and bullets. Everyone is running back and forth. We dig ourselves deeper holes in the ground. I grab my children. I am allowed into one of the dugout hiding places after I reminded the people that my husband had built that very same hiding place in just one day when he was here the last time. That is why I was allowed to stay there.

We jump into our secure hiding places; it is extremely crowded inside. Everyone is frightened and that causes us to feel less secure. We fall down as if we are torn to shreds; we don't even know where we are in this world. My husband then left to fight with the partisans.

The earth was wet when we all ran into the dugout hiding place. It was very crowded with eight people. We all had to lie on top of each other. The air was choking and foul smelling. But at night we would open the little door and allow some fresh air to enter. I could not eat. Then when we were on the verge of passing out, we were able to survive but with a few peas to eat. This lasted for two days and three nights.

It became quieter, but for us other troubles began. In that hiding place the situation became worse and we had to abandon it. I remind myself that it was already springtime. The earth was wet. Our hiding place became infested with crawling worms, and from hunger we all became very weak.

◊ ◊ ◊

At night we would make a fire from small pieces of wood. We would wring out our clothing over the fire so the lice would fall into the flames. The partisans taught us how to do that. But the lice had already infested us and ate at our skin. We began to feel sick; some of us had typhus, others came down with awful itching.

I came down with a severe case of itching that made me jump around. I smeared myself with some tar and also my children so they would not suffer. But my little boys did suffer and shortly after my older boy came down with a fever. He had a high fever; you could feel that his body was on fire. He is just lying there, very hot with fever, like a fire has engulfed him. What can I do? Where can I find a doctor? How can I save him from dying? I understand that he is sick and has succumbed to typhus, an epidemic that is rampant in the forest.

God in Heaven, what should I do now, how can I save him? I saved both my children from the fire (*meaning the German's bullets*). From the frost, I warmed my children's feet at my bosom. To save ourselves from death, I jumped with both my children into the hiding place. God in heaven, show me the way; have pity on us. I see that my little boy is burning up. His small lips are dried up. My poor child, how can I save you? I pour cold water on him and shake him, and ask him, "My dear son what do you want?" He cannot speak. But a little while later he says, "Mother, I want an egg. If I had an egg I would not be sick; I would become well right away." The child's request was for a little bit of milk or an egg. He was having a dream in his mind.

The request was a child's dream. I took him to my bosom and told him a story. The story was that somewhere there is a free country where people could go out and buy and pay for anything they wanted, and where you can eat more than just one egg. From afar my other little boy heard the story, and with a heartfelt sigh, fell asleep. I felt that the free country, the free world, was only a dream and that we would never live to see it.

(I remember this incident like it was a dream. I was very hungry and I was lying down speaking with my mother. My thought was that food such as an egg would make me well again. – H.M.)

I wait and it doesn't take long for my second child to become sick. I look at my two children. Who is guilty of making you suffer so much? Why did I bring you upon this earth? God is punishing me for trying to survive, but we are innocent as the world is my witness.

◊ ◊ ◊

I think and talk to myself like my old aunt. I wake myself up and talk to myself and want to die. I have forgotten about my home and the loved ones that I knew. I am told that this person has been killed, that other persons have fallen or died; the teenage boys who are the partisans in the forest are being shot. I am dumbfounded. I cannot speak. This has a profound effect on me. I don't care anymore about anything. My thoughts were that the dead ones have it good, because they are not suffering any more. When will I be free from all my *tzorehs* (troubles)?

My husband began to search me out among the folks from Zhetel, the people from our same village that were sitting separately. They did not want to have anything to do with me because I had small children with me. So I had to sit by myself with my children. These were very bitter circumstances. We lost many of our good friends from the forest; very dear pitiful *boychikez* (young men), from hunger. At every step we would hear that many of us have been killed.

I look at myself and my children. God in heaven, answer me. I want to make an end of this. I will find someone who will shoot me. The children are hungry. They are crying as I hold them and promise them food. But what food can I offer them? I would get an answer from the Russian commanders. I would ask for bread for my two children. The Russian commanders would answer that their wives were already dead. They did not speak anymore about this. Any speaking about it would serve no purpose.

There were no doctors. Then I did hear that a doctor was brought in that was serving the Russian partisans. He was a Jewish doctor. The partisans risked their lives and brought the doctor all the way from Lida. He was Dr. Mesnik. But what good is a doctor without any medication, without a little bit of milk for the children and without food or warm clothing? Now I run to people, strangers that I see. I ask them to save me or to give me some advice on how I can survive. But they have the same problems and I have children so they don't want to be near me. What can I do being here now?

I can rely on a miracle to happen. I don't know how to tell the story of my sick children. Should I come right out and ask for a doctor for my sick children? But the doctor would need medicine to treat sick children. Would people believe me? I don't even believe myself. I must break free of that kind of thinking.

My eyes are wet from crying and yelling. My children appear like very skinny sheep that were chased away from a warm home that once belonged to them. They are outfitted in little girl's clothing, little jackets that I sewed myself. Their legs are like little thin sticks from a tree. There were no other children and no one wanted to deal with me. Their mother held them to her bosom and created them out of love, and the mother's heart healed them, kept them warm and with love made them full and took away their hunger pains. My husband did not know about my children's terrible illness.

In the meantime, I became the foolish mother in the forest. Who keeps two small children? "My children were killed; I could not keep children here," another mother tells me. My two small children overhear this in the forest. What can my children do?

I think that to me my children are heroes. Grown up people who have lost their lives are heroes, but my children remain alive. Why do I want it this way, I am asked? I feel foolish and when I answer that I want to save my children, I was made to feel like a fool for wanting to save my children.

The area around us is a mixture of artillery, gun powder and all sorts of weapons. There is no one to call out to. All the roads are blocked off. The only way left is to go deep into the ground; that is what we thought. I beg God, "God in Heaven, take me away. I cannot suffer any more."

The firestorm has become a little less intense. The sky is red. We are waiting for the day that we will be freed from death.

The ground is our best friend because it provides us a place for shelters. We haven't found a new hiding place yet. We became like animals; we forgot about civilization. Before my eyes, not far from where I lay in the forest, was a Jewish cemetery. What does this Jewish cemetery in the middle of the woods mean? Buried there are those who died from frostbite on their feet and those that the Germans had shot. The bodies were placed in one area because the ground was too hard to dig up. The human remains were scattered by the forest animals. To write and describe this scene is impossible.

◊ ◊ ◊

My husband arrived to help us. He was unable to see us for a few months. He survived some terrible ordeals. He and the other partisans were chased and they fell into water. They were able to elude the Germans who were now located far away. Individually the partisans hid out and became separated from the partisan leader. More than half lost their lives to the White Poles.

(It was a known fact that the White Poles, also known as Armia Krajowa (AK), were supplied by the Germans, except for food. The AK soldiers obtained food from the local peasants.[1] – H.M.)

My husband found his way back to the forest where we were hiding. He had been told that his wife Shanke was seen lying dead together with their children. They described that I was on the ground with my long hair disheveled; both my eyes were picked out by crows and one of my hands was torn away.

Also the children were lying dead in a frightful position and condition.

That is why my husband did not hurry back to see if we were alive. His eyes did not believe when he arrived and saw us all sitting and all alive. I now want go with my husband, but since I had children, that was impossible. But he also sees the problem that has befallen us. The children and I are very sick.

◊ ◊ ◊

It soon becomes nighttime. The night is ours and is also good for us. When I was a young girl, I would wonder why we needed the nighttime. The daytime was much better than the night. But how were we to know that now the nighttime is our best time? Most nights we survived by sitting by the open fire and even quietly singing songs to ourselves to make us feel better. The birds and all those of us that escaped became like one family in the forest. The forest did not carry our voices far, but rather engulfed us and helped us.

◊ ◊ ◊

After a storm comes the calm. We become used to the big troubles, but the situation changes. Time does not stand still, but continues to run. Bitter cold days drag on. There are a few people left; survivors after many months of continuous casualties. You could count on your fingers the number of people that are left.

And what do you think I can do for my two children? My children were chased away from their homes, where they belonged, where they walked together with other children and grownups. And now my children crawl around in the forest like wild animals. I am made of iron to endure this.

THE SECOND YEAR IN THE FOREST

I am now in the forest the second year. I am beginning to become familiar with the forest and its behavior. The birds know me. The flies and the mosquitoes have long awaited our pain ridden bodies and our feet. The dirt of our bodies attracts the flies, lice, and mosquitoes; we try not to allow such small creatures to attach themselves to us. There were also leeches to deal with. But the situation becomes worse day by day.

I am told that the lice have become a big problem and cause people to die. An acquaintance of mine, a teacher also with two children who was not far from me, was sick with typhus and was literally eaten by the lice and died. She perished at her place. The children were yelling because their mother was dead. Soon the screaming stopped. Her children died soon afterwards because there was no one to help the children when they cried out by their mother's dead body. And soon the screaming stopped. The partisans told me that they broke down their shelter upon them and buried them.

And that is what awaited me each day – that I should die and be buried with the children in the lean-to.

◊ ◊ ◊

The days were hard and there was no hope. Desperation hung over our heads. We were no longer used to a face with a smile or a laugh. And it was better to be without any news

55

because the news was always very sad. The winter went away, and very few of us remained alive. Spring is approaching. The snow is beginning to melt. We find ourselves in quiet surroundings. The Germans are occupied fighting on the main front.

We begin to get ourselves together. We go out of our dugout hiding places and walk a few miles to the *Goyim* (Gentiles), that is to the peasants that remained. These are Goyim that we could trust and we ask them for some milk and some food. And as I wrote before, everything was done at night.

This time when I left the forest, it was still daylight. Even though it was spring, everything was still frozen, so we had to cross over ice. One other person went with me. We crossed the stillness of the forest through mud and ice. We broke through the ice and we were stuck in the freezing mud. We could not go back nor could we go forward. My friend Chaikah began to cry as she stood in the frozen water over her knees. Something tells me to get out, to get out. I take my friend's hand and we just get deeper into the mud. But to whom do we yell for help? Who will help us? God in Heaven?

We finally crawl out of the mud. Everything on us is frozen. Our feet are frozen and the skin is red from the cold. We both look at each other and say this is impossible. Our clothing is frozen on us. We won't be able to go any further. The question is if someone will allow us in. Where are we going? But the will to live is very strong and prevails.

We enter the house of a peasant. The peasant at first looks at us and says he has nothing to give us. He himself is a wanderer. He knows this place and he has to wait until summer when the mud dries up so people can get here. He was surprised that two young women were able to get through the mud.

The peasant tells us that there is good news. The Germans are taking heavy casualties. He further says that when the German army retreats, they will have to occupy the forest. There is no other road out for them. That is not good news.

(In reality, the Russian Army was quickly advancing west and isolating and annihilating large groups of German soldiers. The Russian soldiers would certainly go after the Germans in the forest and would be aided by the partisans who, being lead by Russian officers, were in communication with Moscow headquarters. – H.M.)

The peasant gives us some bread and some flour. We ate a little bit. But now how do we get back? He tells us to go back by the same route we came, but he is surprised that we did not drown getting there. The peasant makes a joke that soon he will have to hide in the forest because he helped the partisans. "I cannot help you anymore; you must go," he yelled into our faces.

We leave the peasant's house more worried about the cold and the wetness. We start to go back on a different path; maybe there won't be as much water or mud. We walk with large sticks in our hands and go through the lake that was always full of deep mud. I remember that the water was up to our necks. God in heaven, where are you, don't you see how we are suffering?

From afar we see a sad scene. The Jewish partisans are trying to cross the same swamp. The partisans' horse fell through the ice and is deep in mud. Their supplies become wet as they are standing around in mud and water. There are some children nearby who escaped from the Germans. The Jewish children try to get the horse out of the water and mud. With rifles in their hands and hands that were weak, the partisans try to get the horse out of the water.

I finally arrive at my safe place and I see that my children are lying down and are shaking from the cold. I make a small fire and sit my children close by. The firewood is cracking. I hug my children closer to me to give them more warmth. Then I tell them where I was – in a house that was warm inside with an ongoing fire, just like our own home a long time ago. I told my children how a house looks. As I sit and speak, I think about the other children. Who will keep them warm? What will be the outcome, what will be the end of all this?

My older boy has a thought and says, "A house, what does it look like?" I tell my son what a house is. A place that is warm. A place where you can lie down and go to sleep. With his childish mind he thinks that a house is the forest. It is a joke, but my heart aches from that thought.

◊ ◊ ◊

We continue to sit by the fire at night to warm are our hands and cold feet. And if our feet are warm, then our backs are cold. Our clothing is burned; our hearts are cold. So we sit like this with a great deal of time to think. And what do we think about and what comes to our minds? Thoughts of various ways of escaping from the forest are always on our minds. These answers and thoughts were always very natural to us. I would even speak with my little older son and ask him these questions about all our troubles just as if he were a grown-up.

My son would help me bring firewood and also helped saw down a tree. I would get my son's opinion as to which tree was dry enough to burn. He would keep the fire burning and keep the water warm from one day to the next because matches were just not obtainable. My son gains knowledge of the forest and helps his mother.

◊ ◊ ◊

Nature was on our side. We enjoyed the singing of the song birds. The birds were the toys that I should have been buying for my children.

It was hard to keep *Shabbos* (the Sabbath). There are more hardships from day to day, but the weather becomes a little warmer. The earth gives some of its bounty. There are blueberries, red ones and black ones, and mushrooms. We gather them all and we eat. I now have help gathering the berries and mushrooms. My two children are growing up and are becoming like *mentshen* (people, or adults). The little one is three-and-a-half and the older one is now five-and-a-half years old.

GOOD NEWS AND NEW DANGERS

We are now hearing various good news. The German army will not last too much longer. A second fighting front has opened up. We receive this news from the peasants who have come a long way. Better news than that cannot be. It is like being stuck with pins in your head. Is it possible that this is really happening? My mind starts to spin, to think and dream about a bed to lay down with a pillow. This was our wish; to have a home. My hearts beats; the pain is great.

We hear pieces of better news from different people. They come in groups or alone and they are coming closer to us. These are people who have escaped from other small cities and villages near our forest – orphans, lonely people. From our small town very few are left. Each one tells some news, what they have heard and what news we can expect.

◊ ◊ ◊

We are told that tomorrow, by noon, those of us in the forest must evacuate. This order comes from a Russian commander who parachuted into the forest to lead the partisans. I am approached by a Russian officer on horseback and warned that this is a time of war and we must obey orders and evacuate the forest. We can go anywhere within five miles of this place. I tell him that my options are limited because I have two small children. I ask him where can I go that is safe. There are Germans everywhere. We can hear them shooting.

The commander does not care. The forest must be evacuated. And as I speak with him, I see various civilians pack up their meager belongings and start to walk out of the area crying. No one knows what this evacuation means. It does not look good. No one is allowed to ask any questions.

These are Russian orders. You can be shot by the Russians for asking any questions in this situation.

The Russian commander rides away on horseback and leaves us with great troubles and fear; we are going into the fire. Police who are collaborators with the Germans are close by. Where will I go? God should only help me.

It is very dark. I am sitting all alone. Fires are not allowed now. In the dark my eyes are playing tricks on me. I take my children closer as I feel our new danger. It becomes quieter and quieter, but I don't think that anything will happen. My children fall asleep, but I am unable to sleep. I am not allowed to be here. Tomorrow at noon I will be shot; that was the order issued by the Russian commander. I will be shot because the Russian commander had already warned me to leave this place. A Russian bullet is the same as a German bullet. Both will kill you.

My dear friends, I don't blame any of you that you had abandoned me and left me alone in the forest; yes, you wanted to live and to survive. But I want to live also and so do my children. They all ran away from me, afraid that the children would make a noise and give us away. Even now I see them running.

◊ ◊ ◊

The trees are on fire and you have to hold a thick branch over your head so you do not get burned. What should I do? I don't know who the present occupiers of the forest are – the Russian or the Germans? I run here and I run there, but it does not help. The fire makes it appear as if it is daytime, and daytime is for us is an enemy. We know that our enemies would not venture into the forest at night. But the light from the fires makes us targets.

I ask the children to stand up on their feet and yell to them, "Come children, the Germans are here, they are close to us. Let's hurry and run." Half asleep, the children hear my words. The children begin to run, barefooted, blood running down from their torn and bloody little feet.

Slowly my older son and I stopped. I then had my younger son in my arms. In the darkness, I feel the way. I walk as if in a daze, half asleep. I don't know where I am going. In this manner, I walked about half an hour and fell down on the ground by a tree. Here I will remain. I cannot go on anymore. I start to cry, "God in Heaven, give me the end and I will be quiet and at peace." I gathered leaves, placed them beneath a tree and made a *geleger* (sleeping place). With my heart racing and nervous fright in my heart, I wait what the morning will bring.

But I did not have to wait long for the morning. Right away, at the same hour, the sky became red from a big fire not far from me. There were rockets in the sky with various markings. I don't know what I can do. The Germans have already occupied the forest. Suddenly everything is quiet. We don't hear any more shooting. It is a mystery. What is happening here? There is no one around us. The children are shaking. From afar we can hear the Germans speaking in German. "Mother, the fire is coming on our side, the fire is not a good sign," both my little children said.

Even though I have a fever, my mind is working very quickly. Here we will be burned to death, or captured alive.

We will soon be in the hands of the murderers. Everything becomes mixed up in my feverish and fearful mind. I feel like I am a worm, turning from one tree to the next. I want to be a mouse, an animal, or a tree. I want to crawl into the ground. Please give me an *aytzeh* (way out, a solution). My mind works very quickly. My face is flush with blood. I try to figure out who will survive. I see strange colors in the forest. Maybe I can see what is happening. I am accustomed to catastrophes, but now I don't know what will happen. As I lay down, my eyes look up above as if someone from the heavens will tell me something.

I see some daylight coming. The daytime was now a small problem for us. But let this day be an end to all my *tzorehs* (troubles). The day started very quietly. We watched as the sky became pale and the fire blends into the daylight and dissipates. Each day was very difficult, and this day was even more troublesome. I did not see anyone. I was afraid of what will occur to me and the children at noon. I did not leave the forest. I waited for anyone. Perhaps I would hear something from someone. Who remained alive, who survived?

Every sound or noise in the forest would make my hair stand up with fright. And also my children would jump from their places. But it was just my imagination. It was absolutely quiet. Maybe something good will happen. But for me everything was an unknown. I don't know what will happen during the day or the night. I am all alone, an outcast, guilty and sentenced by my own brothers to be alone.

THE RUSSIAN PARTISANS

The Russian leaders that take our side told everyone to leave the forest. I will remember that day. It soon became nighttime. My husband does not know if we are still alive. Later on he tells me that everyone abandoned me and that I was surely set to be shot if I did not leave. It is a question if I am still alive.

◊ ◊ ◊

My husband arrives and does not find me. I went a little further where I made my camp. From that location, I was able to understand various signs. When I finally meet up with my husband, he tells me about a few things that happened. An attack on the Germans was planned by Russian paratroopers. The fire in the forest was to mark the landing points to deceive the Germans. And so finally I received some enlightening news. It was a long time since my heart has such pleasure. Finally we can bring in some bullets and arms to stand up and fight against the Germans. The few that remained alive yelled, "We should take revenge, we should take revenge."

My husband calms me down and tells me that I can remain where I am. More people show up as the good news spreads that we are receiving help in the forest from Moscow. Rumors are going around that it won't be long before the war is over. The Germans have lost, but I always think that we never won anything. We have lost everything. We have lost so many.

So we sit by the fire and begin to speak about sometime being able to go free. And what do I say? We will have to wear sacks over our heads because we all look so bad. How many of us will remain to survive? Will any of us survive? I remember various people that were mixed up: they were homesick, they missed the Jewish *yontovim* (holidays), they were reminiscing about the good times before the war and also remembering about missing a brother, a sister, their children, their mothers and fathers.

We don't know where to run. We don't know which way or where will be better. Nearer or further away? Look how we appear; like people of the forest. Another looks weak, thin and frail with a long neck. But he still has the will to live. But if we are freed, will we be able to live? Can a mother live when her children were taken away from her and before her own eyes sees her children's feet smashed against the wall? Can an orphan live freely and normally if he was brought up in the forest? If we ever arrive in a land where we will be free, we must have in our minds not to forget our dearly loved parents, children, and men and women who perished under these awful conditions.

I went over to another nearby tree and waited for whatever God will bring will be. We were lonely and brokenhearted. We could not get close to anyone. But you and I, my friends from the forest, go home and remember what has happened. That is the wishes of the holy ones that went to their slaughter. We must not forget them and must revenge their blood. We are the only ones and we are the witnesses and we should not remain quiet.

And so with clasped hands, we again sit by the tree as a small fire is burning while dreams are running around in my head. What can we do and what can we say? How can we speak and tell about all this? There are no nice dreams or nice fantasies for us.

◊ ◊ ◊

And then we start again to hear news. Russian parachutists from Moscow descend on forest. One of them speaks little politics, but says that the war will soon end and we will be free, he promises. He left with his rifle, ever watchful for his own life.

The partisans wonder how I could raise two small children and see them grow up in the forest. The partisans speak a great deal with me. I tell them that my children gave me the will and the motivation to live and to survive. To the partisans I am a *geroy* (hero). And the partisans reply that whatever they can do, they will try to help me. The partisans will bring me a few things.

I told the partisans that my children think that a house is a forest. And when I ask them anything about a house they know nothing. We made of joke of this. The Russian captain in the forest asks, "What is a bicycle?" My little son Kalmanke answers, "A large yellow head with small feet." He meant a mouse that was with us in the forest. The Russian officers took great pity on my children and told me that their wives and children were killed.

The Russia soldiers brought bread and meat for the children. I would prepare whiskey for the soldiers. I would obtain the whiskey from a peasant because the peasant knew that it was for a Russian captain and that the captain would come to visit me.

The captain was one of the most important parachutist officers. He told us that three times he had captured and lost the same ground. He was the first one to charge out and take back the lost ground. He is the one that knows best how to combat the enemy. He wears many medals and insignias, one of which says the name Senior Captain. In the meantime, it is quiet from the German side. They are occupied on the fighting front. As the captain speaks I can tell that he is a big anti-Semite and I don't understand why. But he visits me often together with his adjutants.

When people find out that the captain is coming, they come from around the area and gather together and they ask him many questions. The captain knows how to speak and answer the questions. He talks about how the war is being conducted. Now his work is to sing and play the harmonica. His adjutants are lonely, quiet Russians, listening to war songs, songs of the heart, every word known by heart. And when the captain would finish singing, he would ask my children, "What does a house look like, and what does a bicycle look like, and a mouse?" He would remember and to mention everything. My children would make him *frayhlach* (happy).

This was already our better times. But everyone was afraid of what tomorrow would bring. Everyone knows that the captain and all his adjutants were anti-Semitic. He looked like a big hero when he was riding his horse. The captain would guard and oversee everything that went on in the forest.

Day in and day out different occurrences would be heard about the war, but we don't see an end.

MY HUSBAND IS VERY SICK

For a long time my husband was again unable to come to see us. He and his fellow partisans tried to fight in many areas. But each time they returned home, there were fewer of them. Many of the partisans were shot and lost their lives. Furthermore, in each partisan fighting *atraid* (regiment), epidemics broke out. Everyone became sick with typhus. And knowing the weakness of the partisans from the typhus, the Germans took advantage of the situation and *hoben zeh befallen* (attacked them). The Germans would capture the partisans alive and torture them.

One day, early in the morning, I hear talking and then I am called by name, "Shanke," in a soft voice, "your husband is coming." My husband could hardly hold himself up on his feet. He was sick with typhus and had a fever. We had just recently gone through the same illness with the children. What can I do now? Who can I rely on for help? Our own partisans wanted to get rid of those who were infected. The epidemic was cause by all the *shmutz* (filth) and unsanitary conditions.

My husband was sick with a high fever and had been chased out of the partisan camp. He could hardly walk. Germans attacked him. He was able to grab hold of a wagon and hid in the wagon that traveled part of the way. The rest of the time he hid in the forest. He barely made his way through the trees to our area.

The Germans would always know to attack the places where the partisans would be. The Germans chased and captured the partisans, even the sick and the crippled. There was almost nothing left of the partisans. Some of the partisans committed suicide, rather than being captured into the hands of the murderers.

Our skin burns with fright, what do we do, where do we go? The Germans have rifles and arms, but what do our weak, hungry and sickly partisans have?

My husband could no longer go inside our lean-to. He lies on the ground. The children are around him, but they don't recognize him. His voice had dramatically changed. The children speak like little birds; better that they should go away. My husband lies there, not knowing where he is; his mind elsewhere. He speaks a little from his fever; I don't know what he is saying.

Some Russians arrive and tell us that the Germans are losing. The Germans are close by, but they are losing the war. We are waiting for the Germans to run into the forest and in such a case, we were all afraid.

It appears that the Germans have begun to suffer on the fighting front. They began to withdraw from their positions. They wanted to occupy the forests.

The same night, not knowing what is happening, I did not know what to do with my husband. His color is yellow and he is lying stretched out on the ground on some sticks. He doesn't speak.

In the forest, I "hear" a dead silence. The forest is our witness of trouble. And from the silence became a change. We struggled this way for some time.

My sick husband is lying on the ground with fever. The children still don't recognize him; they hide near and behind him. A gray wetness is descending over the forest. It becomes quiet all around us. But I cannot be quiet myself. I don't know what tomorrow awaits me. The situation is strained. But now it is still quiet.

All of a sudden, the silence is broken from a nearby shot, right by our lean-to. My husband got up and grabbed his rifle. The children and I embraced each other and stood beneath the rifle. We stood that way for a long time. We did not know who fired the shots over our heads. The night was feverish. We could not talk. Each one of us was going over the last minutes of our lives. I thought that tomorrow was our last day.

NIGHTMARES

The whole night my head was coming apart as I was seeing a terrible scene in my mind. I was seeing my husband being taken away and my children being torn from my arms. My thoughts and dreams were that the Germans found my hiding place and that they are allowing me to stay one more night. Then tomorrow, they will deal with me like I am the biggest criminal. I am suffering, my dear ones, but I may survive. Please tell me which death did I earn?

I endure the dark night with the fever. It is cold and my children are sleeping little by little with big sighs to the sky. I pray to God. The children's little shoes are torn. Everything became rotted. Our skin is cut from the sharp leaves and sticks. What can I do? I am all alone. God should only help me.

Nothing helps me. Wild illusions wear me down. All these times I have *tszores* (troubles). And now before my eyes I have more wild illusions. I am being stuck with knives; my flesh is being torn to pieces. Then I see that ten dead people, not just one, are thrown into the river. As we watch with our own eyes, we are all awaiting the same fate.

My children's eyes show that they want to live and their father should live. My strength is dwindling and I become weak during the long night. I had some very wild thoughts that I would shoot myself in the eyes. I was barely able to stand on my frozen feet. I had very little strength left. And from my weakness, I quickly fell asleep for a short while.

I dreamed that everything was falling apart from me. I had terrible dreams. The forest and the children are being torn away from me. I yell in my sleep. I would ask for *"Nekome, Nekome"* (Revenge, Revenge). In my mind I thought that my children would be torn away from me, and I became half crazy. I did not know what to think or what to do. I saw unbelievable scenes before me. My children are being held by their necks. As I try to take back my children, my hands are ripped off and then my children's hands are torn away. My spirit inside me says to scream out loud, to become wild. My husband and my children became afraid from my screaming and woke me up.

The entire dream took only one minute. That dream I will never forget.

I am burning like a candle. Everything around me is burned. My body, I see, is standing and fighting with itself. A wet sweat engulfed my head and I had convulsions.

The night is ending. My friend is now the daytime. It appears to be a different day. It is very quiet, so quiet that not even a bird showed up to sing its song. I wait for anything to happen, and I wait.

The day was very quiet. But when we ventured out we were all drained. That same evening more partisans from around our part of the forest arrived and gave us the news that a second fighting front is beginning. That means that maybe we will have *mazel* (luck) and survive. It won't be long. Yes, I think to myself, how can this be?

HIDING AND LEAVING NO TRACE

Each day comes and goes. We live on the edge, precariously. The moment I hear any unusual sound I become frightened. My hair *shtait kapayreh* (is disheveled, wild). Shooting is going on for no reason. We don't know where our enemy is and we don't know those who are hiding out with us. That is the worst thing that can happen.

My husband tries to stand on his feet and looks around to find a piece of bread and maybe something else to trade. It did not take him long, and we abandon the place in the forest where we were staying.

We looked for another place to stay, a place that would be closer to a peasant from whom we could get something to eat. We all cried our eyes out. Then each one of us had to camouflage, mask and hide the place where we were. We had to use sticks, moss and leaves to cover our tracks so it would appear that no one was here. When our enemies came to search, they would not be able to find any trace of us ever being there.

Each shovel of dirt to our hiding place was placed in a sack and taken far away to deceive our enemy. In that way the Germans would not find the entrance where I and my children were hiding. My children also helped carry away the dirt on their weak little backs. My children spoke to me and said,

"Mother we want to live. Will we will survive in our underground hiding places?"

So I ask you my dear ones, let us carry the dirt and let us hope that those of us that survive, in our minds we should not forget those who perished and what was done to us. We did not know that we could hide and be lucky to escape from the hands of our murderers.

◊ ◊ ◊

When the Germans had to retreat from the forest, they will not leave any tree or bird. It is terrible. But we are doing what is needed. The new hiding place was finished with lots of help and thanks to my husband and his hard work and strong will. He planned that the entrances should be through a small tree that will be opened as the tree is bent. The second entrance was also through a bent tree. On the path to the entrance, we made a broken tree with many broken branches to camouflage everything. It was so well hidden that we would have a hard time finding the entrance. Inside there was water in the ditch and some dry areas. In an emergency we would run inside.

(When the alarm was sounded that Germans were approaching, I recall picking berries and not paying attention to the danger. I was grabbed by one of the women. I still remember her name – Riveleh. She pulled me into the hiding place through the evergreen tree that acted as a disguised trap door to one of the entrances. We stayed there all day and partially into the night before it was safe to venture out. When we came out, we saw that the Germans had burned anything

that resembled a shelter or lean-to. By the still burning embers of the fire, we baked potatoes. This was our meal for that entire day. – H.M.)

I would feel more alive in our new hiding place. During the day when it was quiet, we would sit at a second place; our main hiding place is a little further away. We would try to think about how to obtain some food and also how to extract some *nekome* (revenge). We wrung our hands nervously. The dirt is all over. The mosquitoes are eating us up alive. We are hopeful of any news that we hear.

The Russian captains in the forest are going around happy. They are counting the weeks that we will be liberated. Everyone asks if they hear any news. Now it is good. Others say the Germans will retreat and go into the woods. The German army would try to go on the big highway, but they would not be allowed through, so they will attempt to hide or go into the woods. There the Russian and Jewish partisans will be waiting to wipe them out.

(Those German soldiers that managed to escape the Russian army's advance westward, by retreating into the forests of Belorussia, at times stumbled into partisan camps and met a torturous and vengeful death at the hands of the partisans. – H.M.)

THE WAR IS OVER

From our hiding place, we hear an old Russian peasant woman who is picking blueberries, yelling in Russian. "You can come out now. The war is over. The Germans have fled." Still not seeing us, she repeats this several times.

We don't know where to go. The Russian captain appears and tells us that we can go out on the main road and greet the Russian tanks that are advancing towards us and continuing the battle against the Germans.

(My mother's memoirs abruptly end here. Our experiences of our liberation from the forest, our return to our home and subsequent journeys, first to a Displaced Persons (DP) camp in Germany and then finally to the United States, are presented in the following pages.

Not mentioned in my mother's memoirs was that my father had the foresight to build a special hiding place as soon as the Germans first occupied our shtetl and weeks before any of the killing began. My father built the hiding place in an area he knew the Germans would never investigate because of the hygiene habits of the Germans. Our hiding place was built under the floorboards of the toilet in our home. This clever piece of ingenuity saved our lives. Of course, there were many other instances not mentioned or forgotten, where my mother's sharp wits kept us alive. – H.M.)

PART II

TRANSLATOR'S MEMORIES

AFTERMATH OF THE WAR

LIBERATION CELEBRATION

An old peasant woman was picking berries and knew we were hiding nearby. She yelled out in her peasant Russian that the Germans are gone. She said it loudly several times. We cautiously left our hiding place to question the old woman. The word filters down that the Germans have officially surrendered. We are finally liberated in early July of 1944.

My father met us in the camp for women and children. We started to walk back to our home in Zhetel. Now we were free to walk on the road, but we were cautious as we headed home.

My father was dressed in what the Russians soldiers would recognize as a typical Russian partisan uniform, not a retreating German soldier's uniform. Though he had blonde hair, he spoke Russian fluently, so the anti-Semites among the Russian soldiers might not identify us as Jews.

The first Russians we saw were in a tank convoy, heading west. My father hailed down the tank commander and the tank stopped momentarily. My father had buried a bottle of vodka, hoping someday to share it with our liberators. He offered the tank commander a drink. The other tanks stopped nearby. The vodka is shared and quickly consumed. My mother, brother and I sat quietly. The Russian officer thanked my father and said he had to leave and continue his mission. There were still many German soldiers to be dealt with. My father saluted the officer and we continued our trek home.

It was that same day that I remember my family still walking on the main road to our *shtetl*, when I saw a column of German prisoners, maybe eight to ten abreast. They were marching east, in the opposite way that my mother and father were going. My father was curious and asked one of the Russian guards where they were taking the prisoners. I very clearly remember the answer in Russian, *"Na Sabir."* In English it means "towards Siberia."

RETURNING HOME

Upon arrival in Zhetel, we find that our home is still standing. We learn that it was used as a headquarters by the local German bureaucrats. The house is empty with the exception of a few scattered tables and chairs. However, there is ammunition everywhere, from small arms bullets to very large anti-aircraft type shells. Not aware of the danger, my brother and I played with the ammunition until our parents took them away. Later on, the Russian authorities came and removed all ammunition from our home.

As a child I recall that the word "*Nemetski*" meant danger or something bad. As my proficiency in the Russian language became better, I found out that the Russian word meant "German."

AN ATTEMPT TO LEAD A NORMAL LIFE

My parents tried very hard to restore the way our house was before the war. We needed everything – beds, furniture, cooking utensils, and above all, food. Food was the most scarce of the commodities. To obtain food and other hard-to-come-by items, my mother and father began to deal in the black market, where you could get practically anything.

My parents were dealing in salt. I remember it was a pale red and pink color. Salt was rationed, but if you had either money or something to trade, you could make a deal with my parents. Dealing in the black market was illegal, but the Russian authorities ignored it – some of them were obtaining their goods from the black market.

Soon their black market business was thriving, but neighbors became jealous. My father was blonde, so most people assumed he was a Christian, not a Jew. It did not take long before my mother and father were discovered to be Jews. There was still a great deal of anti-Semitism in Belorussia and its surrounding areas. Being Jews, and dealing in the technically illegal black market, created a problem for the Russian authorities and eventually for us.

MY FATHER IS APPOINTED FIRE CHIEF

My father had excellent mechanical credentials. The skills came to him naturally. He had a Russian chauffer's license, second class, which meant that he could not only drive any kind of vehicle, he could also repair those vehicles. Before the war, he had gone to a Russian school to learn the skills to qualify for this special license. Also before the war, my father and his brothers ran a bus company with several Studebaker buses. The Russians required this knowledge and experience since there were no vehicle repair facilities in those times.

To prepare for the partisan battles, my father and some other partisans were able to restore a light tank taken out of the Schara River.[5] This tank played an important role in the battle to drive out a German battalion from Nakrishuk for the second time. My father worked with a team of other survivors from Zhetel and other towns to ultimately repair and remodel three light tanks that were recovered from the Schara River.

(My father's name and his special mechanical skills to repair light tanks are mentioned on page 277 in the book by Moshe Kahanovich, "Der Yidisher onteyl in der partizaner-bavegung fun Sovet-Rusland," published in Rome and New York, 1948. – H.M.)

When we returned to our village after the war, a fire station was quickly established. Because of his qualifications and experience, my father was appointed the fire chief of Zhetel.

I remember my brother and me visiting the fire station often to bring my father a hot meal that my mother would prepare. We would play on the fire engine and speak with Chaika, my father's secretary, and also a survivor from Zhetel. I recall the unique smell of gasoline at the fire station. Even now I associate the smell of gasoline fumes with that fire station.

CLOSE CALL WITH A RUNAWAY SLEIGH

Several months after our liberation, an early snow fell in our village. There was over three feet of snow on the ground and still snowing as I traveled with my father in a horse drawn sleigh. My father had to stop the sleigh to use an outhouse. He asked me to hold the horse's reigns and wait for him. Something or somebody spooked the horse. The horse took off with me inside the sleigh. I did not know what to do to stop the horse. From the side I see my father running, barely holding on to his pants. He caught up to the horse and sleigh and was able to take control and stop it. My father saved me from getting hurt or even killed.

MY MOTHER'S REVENGE

My mother had a beautiful prayer shawl that women in the *shtetl* wore on special holiday occasions. Upon returning home after our liberation, my mother tried desperately to put her life back together. Her emotional wounds were very deep. One day while in the marketplace, she saw a peasant woman wearing her beautiful prayer shawl. The peasant woman had made the prayer shawl into a dress. As soon as my mother recognized that it was really her prayer shawl, she began screaming at the peasant woman, and began to tear off the woman's dress. My mother was in a rage, but she was stopped by the local men and women. That did not satisfy my mother. She went to the local police and reported that her shawl had been stolen. The police later returned it to my mother.

My parents were reported to the local authorities that they were dealing in the black market to obtain food and other necessities. It was technically illegal in Russia, but most of the time people looked the other way. However, anti-Semitism still existed. The fact that my father was a Jew made him a marked man.

As the town Fire Chief, my father had contacts in the local government. One of these contacts told my father that his name was on a list to be deported to Siberia for dealing in the black market. In those days in Russia, there was no "due process" or appeals. If your name appeared on the list you were taken in the middle of the night and you were on the way to Siberia.

My father knew he had at the most three days to get away before he was sentenced and deported. He had a Russian soldier's uniform and spoke fluent Russian. He obtained forged papers that indicated he was taking his German war bride and her two small children back to Berlin to meet her family. My mother spoke fluent German. It was very common in those times for Russian soldiers to take German war brides.

We left by horse and wagon the next night. We passed the border checkpoints without any trouble and arrived in Bialystok, Poland, the first major city as we traveled west. We stayed in an apartment in Bialystok for a few months. My parents were still dealing in the black market together with some friends they had met in the partisan groups.

Then we took a train to Warsaw. I remember that it was in the middle of the night. Our papers were checked again and we passed through the checkpoint. At the railway station, Kalmanke, my little brother, saw the train and became frightened and started to cry. He refused to board the train. This was going to create an incident whereby we could be discovered and deported back to Zhetel. Before my brother could make another sound, my father's partner in the black market, a large man, Zavel Mordkowsky, picked up my brother and almost threw him into my mother's arms. She was already on the train. My brother fell asleep and we continued to head west toward Warsaw.

We arrived in Warsaw in the morning. My parents and their friends were constantly dealing in the black market. That is how we had enough food and some clothing.

I remember Warsaw as a city full of rubble and debris. Passageways were cleared where streets once were, allowing at least one lane of cars or trucks to get through. My mother was making extra money as a street vendor selling her famous *piroshkehs* (honey covered pastries with poppy seeds inside and out). I don't remember where she would bake those honey coated treats. We remained in Warsaw a few weeks.

From Warsaw we traveled by train to Berlin. The German civilians had a highly organized campaign to clear the city. I remember women and old men with wheelbarrows, pails, and children's wagons hauling debris, bricks and other rubble to clear the streets. Very few buildings were left standing as a result of the Allied bombing raids. We did not remain in Berlin long, maybe a week or two. Then again by train, we traveled to Frankfurt *am Main* (on the Main River) where a displaced persons (DP) camp was located.

GOING TO SCHOOL IN POLAND

Our town, Zhetel, was in White Russia, or Belorussia at that time. We crossed the border from Belorussia into Poland on our way west to escape my father's probable deportation to Siberia for dealing in the black market.

We were either in Warsaw or Bialystok when I began to attend a Polish school for refugees. I recall going to the Polish school and I soon became proficient in speaking and writing in Polish. The kids did not like the lady teacher. One day, after a heavy snowfall, some of the kids hid behind trees, waited patiently for the teacher to leave the building and then threw snowballs at the teacher. I don't remember if I joined in.

LIFE IN THE DISPLACED PERSONS (DP) CAMP

After several months of traveling west through Warsaw and Berlin, we arrived at a Displaced Persons (DP) camp in Frankfurt am Main, Germany.

Because most of us had lice, we were deloused, cleaned up, given some clothing, and processed. There were clerical people available who spoke many different languages. We gave them our names, birthdates, the town or city where we used to live, and names of relatives in America, Israel or other countries. We were provided temporary lodging and three meals a day by the Red Cross and other agencies.

◊ ◊ ◊

My brother and I were enrolled in a Hebrew school. That was good for us because we did not have to wait in line with our food pails for our meals. Food was served to the Hebrew school children by the Rabbi and his assistants. We worked hard on our lessons. I always managed to get a "5" on my lessons and class exercises. This was the highest grade. I was proud of my Hebrew school work and I kept my work books with the Rabbi's grade of 5 with me all the way to America. I was a good student and enjoyed learning.

Before we started to attend Hebrew school, we had to stand in line for food. Children were given pails for soup or for other food which they carried home. We hated standing in line. I was seven and my little brother was five years old. One of the games we played after we received our pail of food was to spin the pails over our heads very fast. If you did it too slowly, the food spilled out. This was my first lesson in the laws of physics and centrifugal force. I don't remember if I ever lost any food. But waiting in line was awful and to this day I will not wait in line if I can help it. I usually leave that honor to my more patient wife.

◊ ◊ ◊

I recall one day when Eleanor Roosevelt came to our DP camp and gave a speech. She was accompanied by a large group of people, most likely assistants and reporters. In 1946 Eleanor Roosevelt visited the memorial to Holocaust victims at the Zeilsheim DP camp. She spoke to my Uncle Laybke through an interpreter. In future years, Mrs. Roosevelt would become a strong supporter for the establishment of the State of Israel.

My brother and I would always be happy to receive chocolate or chewing gum from passing GIs. However, we did not know that chewing gum was to be chewed. We thought it was food, so we ate it.

My brother and I started our own business selling tobacco. We would find cigarette butts that the American soldiers would discard. We would pick up the butts and remove the remaining tobacco. We would fill a small tin box with the tobacco and sell it as pipe tobacco to the civilians. In return, we would barter for chocolate bars or small toys.

There were small wagons with metal wheels around the DP camp used to haul supplies. We quickly learned where they were stored and used them to conduct races with German children our own age. These German children belonged to the civilians who worked in the DP camps. Fairly quickly, my brother and I were speaking half Yiddish and half German to communicate with the German kids. The play with the German kids was fun and friendly.

◊ ◊ ◊

My parents were still dealing in the black market and doing well. Business was so good that we and our extended family of survivors were able to move out of the DP camp into a small home nearby. My father was able to obtain a small truck and make good money hauling merchandise and people.

Getting automobile tires was a problem because rationing was still in force. My father began dealing in jeep tires. I remember when our home was raided by the American Military Police (MPs). Somebody must have tipped them off. The MPs found some jeep tires in the basement, but the serial numbers where cut or rubbed off. When asked about that, my father told the MPs in German that he did not know how the tires got into the basement. My father did not speak English at the time and he kept shaking his head, saying in German that he did not understand and did not know anything. Actually, as a precaution, he had obscured the tire serial numbers so the black market transactions could not be traced back to him.

ON THE BOAT TO AMERICA

We remained in the house near the DP camp until my aunt, my mother's sister in America, found out through the Red Cross that we were alive. My Uncle Max and Aunt Helen Goldfeder sponsored us to immigrate to the United States, namely to New York City. We left the port of Bremen, Germany, on the ship the Marine Marlin on August 22, 1946.

There were many other refugees on the boat with us. Some were not accustomed to sea voyages and became very sea sick. My brother and I became slightly sea sick, but it only lasted for a day.

I remember that there was plenty of food to eat. We had always used salt and sugar as bargaining commodities. On the boat we saw salt and sugar dispensers on each table in the cafeteria. Almost instantly, the other refugees began to make paper cones and would spill the sugar and salt contents into separate paper cones. It was supposed to be used later on for barter, as they were accustomed. My parents knew enough that we should not do this because it would be like stealing. Besides, there may be new rules in America and we should not embarrass ourselves by the behavior of the other refugees.

My parents befriended an elegant middle-aged couple with no children. They were college educated people. In preparation for our arrival in America, they taught us some basic English phrases like thank you, good-bye, hello, and how do you do.

When we arrived in New York Harbor on September 16, 1946, we were met by our sponsors, my Uncle Max and Aunt Helen, and another close friend from Zhetel, Max Kivel, who came to the United States before the war. It was a very *fraylach* (happy) reunion.

I remember my Uncle Max treating us to our first Coca Cola. My brother and I quickly figured out how to drink the dark carbonated soda using a straw. We were now in America.

IMMIGRANTS IN AMERICA

The first big obstacle for my parents was the language barrier. They enrolled in night school to learn English and to study for the tests they needed to pass in order to become United States citizens. English was a difficult language for them since words were not always written or read they way they sounded. As older students, studying and learning was challenging for them.

My aunt immediately enrolled my brother and me in a New York City public school. I recall that we were first assigned to classes with younger children as we knew very few English words. Fortunately for us, the principal of the school assigned us to a homeroom teacher who understood some Yiddish. Within three months, we were speaking English fluently and helping our parents translate wherever we went, or when they received letters written in English. By that time, I was promoted to a class appropriate for my age, as was my brother.

◊ ◊ ◊

My biggest enjoyment was to help my father listen to the news of the day. I translated the news from English to Yiddish as the announcer read it. The Yiddish radio stations broadcasted at odd hours and by that time my father was already asleep from a hard day's work in a wood cabinet factory. Another program my father enjoyed watching on TV was *Dragnet*. I would also perform a running translation.

My mother was eager to acquire American friends. As a result of these relationships, her English became proficient after about six years. However, my parents' close friends were other refugees who also survived the war. We spent a great deal of time with them, enjoying picnics and parties. It was as if they were trying to make up for lost time – the time taken away from them during the war years. My parents helped sponsor several of their friends to come to the United States. Some would arrive and live with us until they could find a job and a place to live.

◊ ◊ ◊

My brother and I lived in two different cultures. After school, we played stick ball, stoop ball and other street and sidewalk games with our newly-made American friends. In the evenings, in our small Bronx apartment, we reverted to the culture of our *shtetl*. We spoke only Yiddish and ate traditional Eastern European Jewish foods, such as matzo ball soup, kreplach, kugl, and blintzes. When we left our apartment, my brother and I enjoyed frankfurters, ice cream sodas and candy, which we could buy for just a nickel.

My brother and I rarely spoke about our wartime experience. My brother was too young to remember much and I did not make an effort to recall our survival. We were in America. No one was chasing us, we were safe, we had a nice place to live, there was enough food, and we became typical American kids.

◊ ◊ ◊

For years after we arrived in America, my mother had terrible nightmares about our life in the forest. Even as she became older, the nightmares did not go away. At times, she had to use an automobile safety seat belt wrapped around her and a mattress to keep from falling out of bed when those terrible dreams appeared.

BACK IN TIME
THROUGH A CHILD'S EYES

As I read and re-read each page from my mother's memoirs, I am transported back in time to relive some of the incidents. My memories are from the eyes of a three to seven year old child whose seriousness of our life and death struggle in our small village and in hiding in the Belorussian forest was not fully understood until later in my life.

As I get older my memory is fading, but the events that I write about stand out as if they happened just yesterday, while others are just a young child's scattered recollections.

THE GERMAN OCCUPATION OF OUR TOWN

I remember sitting by the window of my home in our town, Zhetel. I was about three years old. I saw two German soldiers in uniform walking together across the street. It must have been spring or summer, because they were not wearing heavy coats. They were carrying weapons; not long rifles, but short weapons. I just watched. It must have been during the summer of 1941 when the German occupation of Zhetel had begun.

THE HIDING PLACE

I have a vague memory of being in a very cramped and dark hiding place. I do remember my little brother being very thirsty and asking for water. There was no water to be had. My grandmother found a small pot and provided some urine for my little brother to drink.

I remember leaving the hiding place and walking in the dark, holding on to my mother's dress or her hand. Although only three years old, I sensed that we were in grave danger. It was important to be as quiet as possible so we would not get caught. We walked through an area that had ground growth, much like poison ivy. The growth was called *kropeveh* and it caused immediate itching when your skin came into contact with its leaves. I was wearing short pants and I could feel the stinging and itching of the leaves on my calves, knees and thighs. At that point I said, "Mother, I can feel the stinging and itching of the *kropeveh*, but I will not cry because I know I have to be quiet."

LEAVING MY LITTLE BROTHER

My mother had a plan to leave my little brother with nuns so at least one member of the family would survive. He was young enough to be brought up as a Christian child and thus might survive.

I remember her leaving my baby brother with the nuns, or outside the nuns' home. My mother and I left. I was able to walk. But then I asked for my little brother, and my mother told me that she had left him with the nuns. I began to cry and said that I missed my baby brother and we should take him with us. My mother also began to cry. We turned around and went back and took my baby brother with us into the forest.

In the previous pages of my mother's memoirs, she writes about this incident in detail. I did not want my little brother to be left alone without us.

REUNITED WITH MY FATHER

I remember looking up from a deep ditch where we were hiding and seeing my father outlined against the sky. He was wearing a combination of a partisan and part of a Russian uniform.

His pants were like those that horseback riders wear. He wore a big heavy jacket. He was holding something in his hands. I remember eating something that he brought with him.

In her memoirs, my mother writes about how my father was able to find us through the help of friendly peasants.

A CHILD'S LIFE IN THE FOREST

My mother would often talk to me about life in a home – a home with heat; a warm place where you could sleep quietly. Since I was so young when we escaped into the forest, I really did not know what a home looked like. But in my child's mind I could relate a home to something else. I tried to make a connection with the forest mice and a home. I was asked in a joking manner by one of the visiting Russian partisans if I knew what a house was. I was already speaking Russian fluently, so I said that a house is something with *balshaia galava y malynki noshki* (a large head and small feet). That created a great deal of laughter, which was often needed to break our gloomy situation.

Another time I saw the men playing cards. I said that I would also like to have some cards to play with. Since I was already about six years old at the time, I was given a penknife and some tree bark from which I could fashion playing cards. I remember whittling down the red tree bark and finishing two cards before I cut myself. That ended my goal to make an entire deck of playing cards.

A VERY CLOSE CALL

It was a beautiful spring day. The sun was shining. Together with other Jewish survivors in the forest, I was picking ground berries. All of a sudden the alarm was sounded that a German patrol was nearby and coming in our direction. As a five year old child busy picking delicious berries to eat, I was absorbed in that activity. I did not realize the danger. One of the young women, whose name I still remember, Riveleh, grabbed me and pulled me down into our underground hiding place. I still remember Riveleh pushing back the trunk of a small tree, which opened to a tunnel, and pushing me into the tunnel. She followed after she had closed the tree so it would be camouflaged and appear as an ordinary tree. I knew already to lie very still and not to say a word. We could hear the Germans above ground. The Germans destroyed everything and would burn any structure that they would find, especially our *zemlyankas*.

That night we emerged from our underground tunnels. We knew that the Germans would not return to the same place at night. We baked potatoes in the smoking ambers of the lean-tos that were burned to the ground. That was our meal that night.

HELPING MY MOTHER AND FATHER

It was now our second year hiding out in the forest. Somehow my mother got hold of a large saw, about six feet long, the kind with wooden handles at each end. Winter was approaching and it was important that we had an adequate supply of firewood. I remember holding and pulling one end of the saw, while my mother was at the other end. We were able to slowly cut logs from dead fallen trees.

From time to time my father would visit the partisan camps where the women and children were located. As a partisan fighter, he was under orders from either Russian or Jewish officers to go out on missions. These missions included mining roads, blowing up bridges and reprisals on informers. My father's other assignments were to take two weapons that did not work and make at least one work.

One time my father carried a Russian-type Tommy gun and a light machine gun. Both weapons had the bullet magazine on top, like a record player. I remember loading those magazines for my father as he prepared to go out on his next mission.

It was always a treat to see my father. He would bring us some food and sometimes clothing. There was never enough food to eat.

MY FATHER TELLS ME ABOUT HIS MISSIONS

My father would share the tactics of partisan missions with me. At age six I was able to understand such things fairly well.

As I grew older, he would give me more detailed descriptions of these missions. He would often be assigned to mine a major road where a German convoy was expected. He worked with another partisan to plant the mine. The strategy was to select a bend in the road so the partisans would not be easily spotted. Then they would wait for the German motorcycle escort to pass. The mine would be placed in the middle of the road by one member of the partisan team and immediately covered with cow manure, which was carried in a basket by the second member of the team.

The partisan team had perhaps 60 seconds to hide before the main convoy would see them. If all went well, the mine would go off when the first heavy German vehicle would detonate it. The partisans would open a barrage of fire from concealed positions and then scatter into the forest.

My father told me about the partisan missions designed to root out informers. The informers were mostly peasants anxious to collect a reward for each Jew that they could turn in to the Germans. On those missions, my father was part of the outside guard and execution squad. These missions were carried out at night in great secrecy. After each informer was executed, a note was pinned to his body. The note said that the partisans will provide the same fate to any informers from now on. The word spread quickly among the peasants and the surrounding towns and villages. The ultimate result was that informers ceased to be a problem and were essentially eliminated.

◊ ◊ ◊

It was spring of 1944. I was already almost six years old. One night I asked to stand guard, but was told I was too young. However, my father showed me his rifle and machine gun. He taught me how to load and shoot it. Since I was very small, I was told to hold the stock of the rifle against a tree trunk when I pull the trigger. Later in the day, when my father was assured there were no threats from nearby Germans, he allowed me some practice firing. We were deep in the forest and away from any danger at the time. The Germans were in full retreat and we were expected to be liberated in a matter of weeks. In reality, it took two or three more months.

◊ ◊ ◊

I remember lying in the forest at night listening to the distinctive sound of the Russian Katyusha rockets. At first I could hear their sounds in the distance. I asked my mother about the rockets. She told me that it was good that each night the sounds of the Katyushas became louder, for it meant that the Germans are being forced to retreat west. As the rockets came closer and closer, we knew that soon the Russians would come to liberate us.

When we would get together with the Russian partisans, they would often sing the popular wartime song, "Katyusha," about a girl longing for her absent beloved, who is away performing military service. I cherish that song and still play it now from time to time.

PART III

A TRIBUTE TO SHLAMKE MINUSKIN AND HIS NEPHEW, KALMAN MINUSKIN

INTRODUCTION

The following pages contain excerpts of my cousin Kalman Minuskin's story of his survival during the German occupation of Zhetel. Most of the information was derived from Kalman's book, *In the Ghetto and in the Forest,* an autobiography written in Hebrew in 1990. [2, 3] I have included some of my own memories and those of my mother in this section.

My father, Shlamke, saved the lives of Kalman's mother and brother by hiding them in the attic of the synagogue during a German roundup of Jews who were to be murdered. My father also had the foresight to plan and build a hiding place. At one point in time, that hiding place saved most of our families from being murdered by the Germans.

The story underscores our family's struggle for survival under the most dreadful conditions. This part is dedicated to the memory of my cousin, who passed away in August 2008 and to my father, who passed away in August 1984.

Harold Minuskin

PLANS FOR A HIDING PLACE

My father, Shlamke Minuskin, was a maverick, a man of action and a very creative person. In September 1939, when news spread in our town that war broke out and the German army was advancing towards Zhetel, my father immediately sensed that our lives could be in danger. My father and his brothers, Myarim (Kalman's father) and Mulka, had built our home and were very familiar with carpentry work. My father's priority was to build a suitable hiding place. It would have to be a place that the Germans would never find or would not want to enter. He built a secret hiding place under an outhouse in our backyard. It was a decision that later proved to save the lives of members of the Minuskin family: my mother, Shanke, my two year old brother, Kalmanke, myself, Henikel, my Cousin Kalman, my Aunt Yoche, and her husband Mulke, and their two children, a son, also called Kalman, and a daughter, Marile, my Aunt Friedka, my grandmother, Dvora, and two boys from the city of Luptz who were related to my Aunt Yoche.

(There were three Minuskin family members named Kalman. They were all named after our grandfather, Kalman Minuskin, who passed away before war broke out. My bother Kalman, was called Kalmanke. The diminutive was used because he was the youngest Kalman. There was my cousin Kalman, eleven years old when the war started, who was the son of Myarim and Batya. There was another Kalman, four years old, who was the son of Yoche and Mulke Minuskin.

My father had two other brothers. Laybke escaped from Zhetel by a train that headed east towards Siberia. He wound up in a DP camp. My parents sponsored him to immigrate to the United States in the late 1940s. His brother, Nyomke (Benjamin), immigrated to Israel before the war. – H.M.)

My father sensed trouble from the Germans. As a man with an independent mind, he ignored the German edict of July 23, 1941, that all men between the ages of 16 to 60 must assemble in the center of the town. Rather than being taken by truck to do "light work," as announced by the German SS officer, 120 of the most influential Jews from Zhetel were murdered and thrown into a prepared mass grave, about 20 miles from Zhetel, near the town of Novogrodok. My father's defiance of the German order to assemble in the town center saved his life.

ORDERED INTO THE ZHETLER GHETTO

On February 22, 1942, the Germans announced a decree that all the Jews must leave their homes and move into a small area of Zhetel, known as the ghetto, within a very short period of time. Anyone found outside of the ghetto after that time would be shot on the spot.

The homes in the ghetto were emptied of all furnishings. This allowed the Germans to build double and triple bunk beds like those used in jails. The purpose was to cram as many people as possible in a room. Since our home was already inside the ghetto, our relatives moved into our home – my Cousin Kalman, his mother and father, and his three brothers (Moshele, Shepsele and Berrele). Other family members also came into our home. They were my Uncle Mulke and my Aunt Yoche, together with their two children, my Aunt Friedka, my grandmother, Dvora Minuskin, and two young boys. We were cramped into very small rooms with triple bunk beds.

In spite of these harsh and frightful conditions, somehow all our family members found a little space for themselves as we tried to live in harmony despite the terrible conditions imposed on all the Jews of Zhetel. Inside our home, there was a great deal of noise from the small children who were running around the rooms. The adults were tolerant and did not punish the children.

Kalman's father, Myarim, and my father, Shlamke, never rested about planning ways to escape from the ghetto. After the first slaughter of Zhetler Jews, they decided to build a camouflaged hiding place in the backyard of our house. Secretly, they dug a hole seven and a half feet deep by six feet wide by six feet long. Wooden planks were placed on the top of the hole and the planks were covered with soil. The plan was to build a wooden outhouse directly above the soil that covered the planks. The outhouse was constructed to appear like any other outhouse of those days. The human waste from the outhouse would fall on the wooden planks covering the underground hiding place. The entrance was through the toilet. Once the hiding place was completed, it provided us with some sense of security.

INSIDE THE HIDING PLACE

On the morning of August 6, 1942, the Zhetler Ghetto was surrounded by SS soldiers and German police. They entered the ghetto from all directions screaming, swearing and shooting. Kalman ran into our hiding place underneath the toilet in our back yard. Inside the hiding place were nine other family members and two boys from the city of Luptz who were close relatives of my Aunt Yoche, all barely crammed into the small space.

Because there was no light in the hiding place, we could not distinguish between night and day. It was constantly dark. According to Cousin Kalman, the children cried constantly and asked for water. There was no other option but to wet their lips with urine. The parents tried to keep the children quiet by placing their hands over the children's mouths. It was always feared that the children's voices would be heard outside, which would seal our fate. Occasionally screams were heard when people were discovered in their hiding places in homes nearby. The days and nights passed slowly.

At night, Uncle Mulke decided to venture outside the hiding place to contact Kalman's mother and father and discuss plans for the escape from the ghetto. It was decided that there was no point in waiting any longer; an escape was planned for Friday night at midnight. We would seek the safest route, towards the direction of the villages where we could hide and then go into the forest. Friday passed by restlessly.

The conditions inside the hiding place were terrible. There was no place to move or to lift a hand or foot. Kalman waited for nightfall so he could be reunited with his parents and brothers. The next day, Saturday, Kalman continued to cry for his parents and brothers. Uncle Mulke decided that we would all leave the hiding place, no matter what. On Saturday night, Uncle Mulke instructed us one by one to exit the hiding place quietly. The plan was to all meet at the Talmud Torah (at the school) and from there my uncle would lead us all into the forest.

My grandmother had difficulty walking and seeing because in the hiding place she was confined to a very small space and it was dark all the time. Aunt Frieda reconciled herself that her destiny would be to remain with my grandmother. They separated from us and were captured and killed by the Germans.

My mother, with my brother in her arms and with me holding on to her dress, decided to go in a different direction. Without adequate food, or water, deprived of sleep, my mother wandered away from our hiding place in a daze. She forgot about the planned meeting place and set off on her own. My mother's story continues in her own words in the section titled "On the Run to the Forest."

KALMAN ESCAPES FROM THE GHETTO

Kalman left the Zhetler Ghetto late at night. He crossed through backyards and climbed fences to get out of town. He continued until he reached the town outskirts. He laid down in a wheat field and fell asleep. He awoke at dawn to the sounds of screaming, crying and shooting from the direction of the new cemetery. As he walked away from Zhetel, the noises continued without end.

An old woman from the town took pity on Kalman and shouted: "Run and escape or the Germans will catch you and murder you as they have the others." Some gentiles shouted in anger: "Why are you running away, sooner or later they will catch up with you. Go back to the cemetery. There you will find your parents and the rest of the Jews from the ghetto. The Germans have already prepared your graves."

Kalman ran without stopping until he reached the village of Chadgelan. There he felt more secure since he was far from the Zhetler Ghetto. He was hungry and thirsty. He snuck into the backyard of one of the village houses and found some water to drink. He found an old dry piece of bread left outside. Then he remembered his father's words that "in times of need we have very good gentile friends in the village of Kaminka; they will help us." A young girl came out of one of the houses. Kalman asked her how to get to Kaminka. She gave him detailed directions and said he could hide in one of the villages and find work as a shepherd.

On the evening of August 9, 1942, Kalman arrived in Kaminka and knocked on the door of the first house. Fortunately, they knew Kalman's father and gave Kalman milk and half a loaf of bread. The home owner begged Kalman to leave because his son was a police officer and would take Kalman back to the Germans. Kalman left, and as darkness approached, he found an open barn. He entered and went to sleep on a pile of hay. The next day, he left quickly with no plan in mind.

Kalman saw a shepherd with his flock in the distance. As he approached closer they both recognized each other. It was Kolya, the son of Kalman's neighbor from Zhetel. He and Kolya were friends from the time they were very young. Kolya comforted Kalman as he realized his dangerous situation and suggested that Kalman stay with him. Kolya would bring enough food for both of them, and they would watch over the sheep together.

Kalman spent five days with Kolya without any problems. Then they saw a young boy in the distance. The boy began to run away. Kalman caught up with him and recognized him as Yankele from Zhetel. He, his parents and other Jews escaped from Dvoretz into the forest. In the dark, Yankele became separated from the group and was not able to find them again. Kolya gave Yankele some water and food, but they had to leave. Kolya told Kalman that they were only one and a half miles from a village and they would be in danger of being discovered now that Kolya was with two Jews.

Yankele and Kalman headed west towards the village of Hiruchz, a journey of about four miles. A farmer greeted Kalman warmly since he remembered trading with Kalman's grandfather, Mordecai Eli Kalbstein. The farmer knew the Germans were murdering the Jews. He also told Kalman that the Germans warned all the villagers that if they were found hiding Jews, their houses would be burned down together with the occupants. In the morning, the farmer gave Kalman a bag with bread, butter, cheese, apples, and milk. He advised Kalman to escape towards the forest of Nakrishuk. The Germans were apprehensive about going into the thick forests.

As darkness fell, Kalman and Yankele approached a house surrounded by a large yard and a fence. They were in the village of Yatzovitch. A man came out of the house carrying an axe and accused Kalman and Yankele of being prowlers. But when he saw them more clearly, he asked who they were. Kalman and Yankele told him of their escape from Zhetel and Kalman mentioned the names of his father and his grandfather.

Thankfully, the man with the axe knew Kalman's grandfather. He took them inside his home and his wife gave them milk, bread and butter, but told them that in the morning they must leave. The man gave Kalman directions towards the forest where they would meet adult Jews. There, in the forest, they would have a chance to survive until the end of the war.

KALMAN REUNITED WITH HIS FAMILY

Kalman and Yankele headed towards the village of Poutishchina, where Kalman was able to steal a pair of wooden shoes for himself. He had been walking barefooted since he had to give up his shoes to bribe a young gentile not to turn him over to the Germans. Even with the wooden shoes, his feet hurt from the wounds caused from walking on stones.

Both youngsters ran away from the village as quickly as they could. When they were a few miles away, they laid down to rest and fell asleep. In the morning, they wandered around looking for a way into the forest. After hours of wandering, they reached a home near the forest. They waited by one of the houses for an hour until the farmer came out. They were afraid to come close because of his dogs, so they shouted from afar that they were Jewish children from Zhetel who were looking for work as shepherds.

The farmer invited them into his home. His wife gave them bread and a bowl of soup. The farmer told them that he was an ally of the partisans. He also told them that many Jews who escaped from the ghetto passed through and that they may even meet with some members of their families who managed to escape from the ghetto. He advised Kalman not to go into the forest on his own since he could easily get lost. He also told Kalman to wait at the outside of the forest until they met up with other Jews. Kalman and Yankele left the farmer and headed towards the forest. They now had new hopes of survival.

After a half hour, Kalman and Yankele arrived at the forest. The forest frightened them since it was very dense. They waited for hours and no one came. From stress and fatigue, they fell asleep. When they awoke the sun was out and two Russian partisans on horseback were standing before them. They were dressed in Russian army uniforms and were heavily armed. Since Kalman managed to learn some Russian at school during the Russian occupation of Zhetel from 1939 to 1940, he told the soldiers of his escape from Zhetel. The Russian soldiers began to interrogate Kalman and Yankele about the villages they had passed through, about the location of Germans, if any automobiles with German soldiers passed by. One of the soldiers allowed Kalman to hold his handgun and said, "In time you will learn to use these arms." The Russians told Kalman and Yankele to enter the forest to search for Jews who also escaped from the ghetto.

(In the following two months, Kalman discovered that those two Russian partisans were Kolya Varchonim, first commander of the partisans in this area, and his assistant, Sasha. – H.M.)

Kalman and Yankele wandered through the forest for the rest of the day. They heard a shout in Russian: "Stop and do not move!" Two boys emerged with rifles pointed towards them. When the two boys saw Kalman's and Yankele's faces, they recognized them and began to speak Yiddish to them. The boys brought them to their group, where they were bombarded with questions. They barely had a chance to answer when Kalman's mother and father appeared and began hugging and kissing him.

Kalman's first question was: "Where are my little brothers, Barrele and Shepsele?" Kalman's mother responded with cries and he immediately understood that they were no longer alive, murdered by the Germans.

MY FATHER SAVES SOME OF OUR FAMILY

Kalman's mother, Batya, told the story of how she was saved but lost her two younger sons, Shepsele and Barrele, when the Germans rounded up most of the Jews from the ghetto. My father did not have the time to run into the hiding place he built near our home and was caught in this round up. Also caught were Kalman's mother, her older son Moishele and her two younger sons.

The Germans transferred everyone into the synagogue, located in the center of Zhetel. The synagogue was used as a transfer station. From there, the Germans forced men, women and children to board trucks. The trucks drove them to the cemetery outside of the western part of the town.

At the cemetery were large long, deep graves that had been prepared a couple of days in advance. Nazi SS officers with machine guns stood along the length of the graves, where they fired upon the Jews.

In the synagogue, from among the crowd of hundreds, my father recognized Kalman's mother. My father, a very courageous man, pulled Kalman's mother and Kalman's brother, Moshele, toward the direction where my father was standing. Unfortunately Kalman's younger brothers became separated from their mother when the Germans grabbed the two children.

My father was familiar with every corner of the synagogue. As a young boy studying the Torah, he would often hide from the rabbi to avoid the lessons. In the noise and confusion, he managed to place a bench in one of the corners and climbed to the attic of the synagogue. Once there he pulled Kalman's mother and brother up with him into the attic. With all the confusion and crying and screaming, the Germans did not notice them. Twelve other men who saw my father go there also climbed up and hid. They all stayed in the synagogue attic until midnight.

When the entire synagogue was emptied and there was complete silence, my father decided to leave the attic and escape. He ordered those in the attic to climb down slowly and led them to the rear exit, away from the ghetto, away from Zhetel, in the direction of the forest. After walking all night, led by my father and Hershel Kaplinsky (who would later emerge as one of the leaders of the Jewish partisans), they arrived in the forest before dawn. Both men were very familiar with the area and that fact alone made their escape into the forest a success.

THE SURVIVAL OF KALMAN'S FATHER

Kalman's father, Myarim, and Kalman's Uncle Ceicile (Batya's brother), escaped from the ghetto on a Friday night.

They thought they would find hiding places in one of the surrounding villages. During their escape attempt, a German patrol noticed them and chased after them. Luckily, they managed to elude the patrol and hid in a wheat field all day. Later that night, they decided to go back to the ghetto to get the rest of the family out. When they returned to the ghetto, they went to the hiding places where they had left their families, but they were gone. They looked in the hiding place that my father built in our back yard below the outhouse, but found it empty. They feared the worst.

After the shock wore off, they decided there was no other choice but to escape into the forest. The escape was not just to save their own lives, but to find ways to take revenge on the German murderers and their collaborators. Myarim was familiar with the route to the forest because of his dealings with the farmers along the way. He owned a grocery store and Ceicile owned a meat store and had good relations with the surrounding farmers. After a few days they reached the forest of Pouschtcha Lipichanite. There they joined the Jewish survivors and the partisan group.

When Myarim and Ceicile met the other survivors in the forest, they were overjoyed to find Kalman's mother, Kalman and Moshele. There was great sorrow when they found out that Berrele and Shepsele were murdered. When Ceicile learned that his wife and children were also murdered in cold blood by the Germans and their collaborators, they all vowed not to rest until they took revenge on the murderers of their loved ones.

PART IV

THE ZHETLER PARTISANS ORGANIZE AND FIGHT BACK

THE MISSIONS

INTRODUCTION

The following material is available because of the efforts of my cousin Kalman Minuskin to help document the Holocaust events in our town of Zhetel. Most of the material was derived from Kalman's book, *In the Ghetto and in the Forest,* written in 1990, plus other reference sources.[2, 3, 4]

The stories represent accounts of how the Jews of Zhetel and other towns were able to organize and fight back successfully against the German murderers and their collaborators.

Harold Minuskin

PARTISAN FAMILIES STRUGGLE TO SURVIVE

The settlement of the families in close proximity to the partisans provided them with feelings of security and the opportunity to receive the occasional food brought by the partisans. However, the concentration of many civilians in one place brought danger to themselves and to the partisan units. The plan was to disperse the civilians into their own groups and away from the partisan fighting groups.

Families and individuals searched for locations where they could hide safely away from the partisans. Life was very difficult for all of them. They were mostly women, children and old men. The young men were part of the partisan units. The civilians' will to survive helped them cope with the bitterly cold Russian winters and above all, their perpetual hunger.

Everyone helped each other build *zemlyankas* in the forest. Some of the shelters were partially underground and partially aboveground. Some were built completely underground to ensure that they would not be discovered by German patrols. The dugout earth was carried many kilometers away to leave no trace of the structure.

All of the shelters were camouflaged above with soil, grass and branches. Only a small opening was left for entry so that the shelter was very difficult to notice, even up close.

The walls of the shelter were built of logs, which were cut down from forest trees. The logs were arranged in a similar manner to a log house with interlocking logs, except that these logs were placed underground.

Inside, arrangements were made for sleeping, the storage of food and a pail for waste. Straw was used for insulation and at times, as a surface to sleep on. This work had to be done over and over again, as partisans kept moving, one step ahead of their enemies.

Everyone cared for themselves according to their abilities when it came to food and clothing. As much food and clothing as possible was saved for winter. In the daytime, everyone hid in the shelters to listen for approaching danger.

The civilians left the shelters at night and went to the nearby villages, sometimes as far as nine or ten miles away, to try to get some bread and potatoes from the villagers. If the villager had a good heart or knew them, he would provide some loaves of bread and a sack of potatoes and even some milk. The food was taken back to the forest before dawn.

◊ ◊ ◊

In the beginning, it was very difficult to adapt to this lifestyle. The civilians found themselves without adequate shoes, shivering from the cold, and frightened from the smallest sound, such as a falling branch or the chirping of a bird. They walked through the forest and fields with their feet unprotected from the rough terrain, the rocks and branches. The pain was felt all over the body. However, it was a must to suffer in silence. No noise of pain was permitted in case someone might hear them and compromise their location to the Germans.

The partisans also concerned themselves with bringing food to their families when they returned from their missions in the villages. At times they would pass by their families and leave them food and sometimes clothing. Other times they would sit around a fire to warm up and tell their families of their experiences. When available, mushrooms collected from the forest were fried in the fire and shared with the group.

◊ ◊ ◊

Life was very hard, especially for those women who had to take care of themselves and their small children. As noted in Kalman's book, this was particularly true for my mother, who had to take care of my younger brother, then only three years old and me, five years old. Our father was away, fighting with the Zhetler partisans, but he would bring us food and some clothing whenever he had an opportunity.

Life was also terribly difficult for those children who were orphans and without any relatives to look after them. These children had a savior, Hertzke Kaminski, from Zhetel. He made it his mission to save the orphaned children. He gathered them together and cared for them with food, clothing and shelter, which enabled some of these children to survive.

◊ ◊ ◊

It was necessary to keep changing hiding places and shelters for security reasons. We were not able to stay in the same place for too long. There were informers, eager to collect rewards offered by the Germans for information where Jews were hiding. With each location change, everything had to be dug up and built from scratch. Generally, the families attempted to keep their shelters a safe distance away from one another, but close enough so that we could maintain contact with each other.

ORGANIZING PARTISAN ACTIVITIES

Prior to 1942, the Jewish partisans operated in segments of small groups of platoons and companies. Each had operated in accordance to their individual desires and abilities as they saw fit. There was no real coordination of any central command or headquarters that gave the groups direction. The tasks of the partisans were noticed in Moscow, where their efforts were recognized as a very positive step towards fighting the Germans.

In the spring of 1943, there was a major turnaround in the organization of the partisans. Moscow sent well-trained leaders, along with supplies and communication equipment, by parachute.

I remember that the white silk of the Russian parachutes were not wasted by the civilians or the partisans. My mother made various types of clothing from the white silk material. In the book, Tank Rider, Into the Reich With the Red Army, by Evgeni Bessonov,[6] the author writes about Russian soldiers who traded parachutes with the local villagers for moonshine and lard. The local villagers sewed the parachute material into blouses and underwear.

The Russian officers who accompanied the equipment took charge of the partisans. They organized the command in a very military-like manner. This increased the morale of the partisans. The partisan activities and operations would now be coordinated under one command headquarters.

The top commander of the newly arrived paratroopers from Moscow was a Jewish general, Davidoff. One of his first orders to the partisans was to protect and support all of the families hiding in the forest. Until that time, the families were spread out, fending for themselves without any direct protection from the partisans. This order had come just in time, as there were some anti-Semites among the Russian partisans who were intimidating and harassing the Jewish families. These anti-Semites blamed the partisan families for any of their misfortunes and failures.

Until this time, the task of the partisans was to operate in small units using such tactics as placing mines in railways, under bridges, on main convoy supply roads, and other methods of attack, which often involved ambushes followed by retreats. With the arrival of Davidoff and the rest of this group came the beginning of organized battles against the Germans, in large forces of partisan battalions and brigades. In this organized manner, the partisans now took all of their orders from one central command headquarters and became more powerful.

The Zhetel Company was incorporated into the Orlanski Battalion, with Kolya Varchonim in command. (Kolya had been the first Russian officer that my Cousin Kalman met in the forest when Kalman escaped from Zhetel.) This battalion was named after the town of Orla, which had been the first to be successfully attacked by a small partisan unit, with great losses to the Germans. The battalion's name was later changed to the Burba Battalion as it grew to accommodate larger numbers of partisans.

Another brigade had been established in the forest, and was referred to as the Lenin Brigade. In command was Valentine Botka, later discovered to be a drunk and an anti-Semite. He was among those who murdered one of the Jewish partisan commanders, Alter Dvoretsky.

One of the Zhetler platoons was transferred to the Lenin Brigade. My father was included in this platoon. The intention was to have at least one Jewish platoon in the Lenin Brigade. It was common knowledge that the Jewish partisans were leaders in the battles, as they were anxious to take their revenge on the Germans. The Jewish partisans were a solid base in the establishment of the partisan movement. Later, another Jewish platoon was included in the newly established Krosno Gwarcheski Battalion.

PARTISANS FROM ZHETEL AND OTHER VILLAGES

The surviving Jews from Zhetel gathered in the Poushtcha Lipichanite forest along with Jews from other surrounding villages and towns such as Zlodek, Belitza, Kazlochena, and Slonim. There were also some Jews who escaped from the ghettos and concentration camps of Dvoretz and Novogrodok.

In the Poushtcha Nalibokete forest, surviving Jews gathered from towns such as Novogrodok, Baronovitch, Lida and other surrounding areas. Together with the Russian partisans who were left when the Red Army retreated, they established a strong fighting force of partisan units in both of the large forest areas.

REPRISALS IN THE VILLAGE OF MOULARI

The partisans began to organize and prepare to take revenge on all who collaborated with the Germans in the nearby areas and in villages on the east side of Zhetel.

The first plan was to reach the village of Moulari to capture two collaborators, Mdzashi and Antone. These two individuals hated Jews. Many of the Jews from Zhetel who escaped from the ghetto were caught by these two men, who threatened them with guns, and then forced them to remove their clothing and give up their valuables. After that, they turned the stark naked Jews over to the Germans. The Rabbi from Zhetel and his wife, who had escaped from Zhetel and were on their way to Dvoretz, were caught by these two collaborators, stripped and returned to the German police in the ghetto. The partisans rejoiced that the time had finally come when revenge could be taken.

On September 10, 1942, a large group of courageous partisans went out in the evening towards the village of Moulari, about 12 miles from the forest and south of Zhetel. After traveling a few hours by wagon, they approached and surrounded the house of Mdzashi. Two of the partisans knocked on the door of the house and asked for him. The response was that he was not at home, but visiting a neighbor.

Despite the danger of being in the area, the partisans decided that they must find Mdzashi. They approached the neighbor's house, which was well lit inside. They could see seventeen people sitting in comfort, enjoying drinks. The partisans pulled out their guns and rifles, entered the house and ordered everyone to raise their hands in the air. Without any hesitation, they pulled Mdzashi from the group and read him his official judgment of the Zhetel partisans loudly and clearly for all the others to hear.

Mdzashi started to plead and beg and swore that the Rabbi was given over to the Germans by his friend Antone and that he himself only gave a few Jews away to the Germans. However, his begging and lies did not help. Everyone knew what part he took in capturing and turning over Jews to the Germans. He was taken outside, put up against the wall, and shot. This was the end of the anti-Semite and murderer, Mdzashi. The same treatment and judgment was given to Antone, with a bullet to his head.

The news of the executions immediately reached the village heads and all of the other surrounding villages. In addition, the partisans posted warning signs: "This action will be repeated against anyone else who collaborates with the Germans."

The gentile population was now aware that there was a fighting force ready to take revenge.

TWO IMPORTANT MISSIONS COMPLETED

During a cold October night, a partisan unit from Zhetel received orders to cut all of the telephone communications between Zhetel and the town of Novialna. Two wagons with four partisans in each wagon began a trip about 11 miles from their base camp to the main road which connected Zhetel and Novialna. There they quickly disconnected the telephone lines.

◊ ◊ ◊

The partisans, all from Zhetel, concluded that they still had enough time in the darkness to carry out another reprisal order before their return to base camp in the morning. The mission was to stop in the town of Maldoush to take revenge on the village head, the anti-Semite Mitosevich. His harassment, capture and return to the Germans of the Jews who had escaped from the ghetto in Zhetel were well known to all.

The partisans arrived at the village and were directed by the farmers to Mitosevich's house. When one of the partisans knocked on the door and asked that the door be opened,

Mitosevich did not comply. Time was of the essence as the partisans did not want to give Mitosevich time to get help from the Germans. The partisans broke down the door and Mitosevitch was taken outside by force with the intention of bringing him back to the forest where he would be given a trial and face justice. However, he fought with all his might and did not make it easy to take him away. His screams and shouts placed the partisans in jeopardy, since they were only a little over a mile from Zhetel. The risk was too great. One of the partisans took immediate action and shot Mitosevitch in the head.

The partisans returned safely to their camp with the satisfaction that they had carried out two successful missions in one night.

COLLABORATORS ELIMINATED IN NOHORNICK VILLAGE

In December 1942, the partisans became aware that the concentration camp in the town of Dvoretz had been liquidated. Most of the Jews there were murdered, with only a few managing to escape into the forest. To the dismay of the partisans, many Jews met their deaths en route to the forest by the hands of the Germans or their Belorussian collaborators, who would turn the Jews over to the Germans.

In one incident, ten Jews who had escaped from Dvoretz came upon a gentile named Bortka from the village of Nohornick. That village was situated halfway between Dvoretz and Zhetel. Bortka and his son managed to persuade the Jews that if they gave Bortka their valuables, he would hide them for a few days and provide them with food and shelter and show them the way towards the forest.

After Bortka put the Jews in a hiding place, he locked the door from the outside, quickly got on his horse and went to the Gestapo in Zhetel where he informed the Germans of his capture of the Jews. The Germans quickly returned with Bortka and murdered the ten Jews on the spot. Bortka and his son received all the clothing the Jews were wearing.

News of this incident reached the Jewish partisans in the forest and an order was given to seven partisans to take revenge on the murderers. One of those partisans was my father.

It was a very cold winter day and the snow fell on the partisans' faces. They traveled in the extreme cold with two sleighs pulled by horses. The trip lasted for a few hours. After the difficult journey, they arrived at the village of Nohornick.

Three partisans remained on guard outside, and the other four armed partisans went into Bortka's house. The partisans took Bortka and his son outside and read them their judgment along with the reasons they were charged. They were both put up against the wall and shot in the head. The partisans attached written notices to their bodies that explained the judgment and the reason behind it.

On the morning of the next day, the story was heard in the villages and the surrounding areas about the end of these two collaborators. It was now understood that the Jewish partisans reach was far and wide and there would be revenge upon anyone taking part in the murder of Jews.

PARTISANS ATTACK ZHETEL POLICE STATION

Following the siege and prior to the partisan reorganization, a group of Zhetler partisans took the initiative to mount an attack on the police station in Zhetel. The commander of the Orlanski Battalion advised the partisans from Zhetel to take advantage of the opportunity that the Zhetler Belorussian police assumed that the Germans had wiped out the partisans and retreated victoriously. Ten partisans went out to attack the police station to remind the Germans and their collaborators, the Belorussian police, that the Jewish partisans were still a force to be dealt with.

Once on the outskirts of town the partisans divided themselves into three groups. At a prearranged time they would simultaneously open fire with automatic weapons towards the police headquarters station in order to create panic.

The police and German soldiers jumped from their beds in panic and confusion and began to run all over the place. As planned, the firing lasted only fifteen minutes. The three groups then met up at a prearranged meeting point and from there proceeded safely back to the forest.

GERMANS ELIMINATED IN RHUDA YAVARSKI VILLAGE

The Jewish partisans continued their task of destroying German strongholds. They also wanted to eliminate the

Germans in Zhetel and in the towns of Kazlochena and Goulodock.

A larger and significant battle took place in the village of Rhuda Yavarski, where the Germans had a large stronghold, their greatest strength and power. Rhuda Yavarski was not far from Poushtcha Lipichanite, located on the main road between Zhetel and Doulodock. The Germans chose this central location as their main stronghold in order to maintain control on the central thoroughfare to prevent the partisans from mining the road and the general area.

At the end of October 1942, a meeting took place of all the commanders of the partisan companies and battalions in Poushtcha Lipichanite. It was decided that a major combined attack of all partisan forces should be planned against the Rhuda Yavarski. The Zhetel Company and a company from the Orlanski Battalion would carry out the main strength of the attack.

The partisan force was divided into three units. Two units took positions as blocking forces on the main roads leading to the village, to prevent reinforcement of German units from entering the village. The main strength came from the Zhetel Company that was to attack the village. At eight o'clock in the morning, the main force entered the village with an armored vehicle in the lead. The partisan forces were equipped with two forty-five millimeter cannons, machine guns and one armored vehicle. This armored vehicle was previously retrieved from the Schara River and repaired by my father and other partisans and was ready for action.

The partisans first announced over a loud speaker that the Germans and the Ukrainian soldiers should raise their hands and surrender, but the Germans opened fire on the partisans from all directions. The armored vehicle returned fire, the signal for the other partisans to attack.

The battle lasted for about an hour. In the end, almost the entire German stronghold and its staff, plus many soldiers, were wiped out – a total of fifty enemy soldiers and collaborators. Many more were wounded and ten were taken prisoner. The partisan losses consisted of two dead and six wounded. A great deal of arms and ammunition were captured and taken back to the partisan base camp.

German reinforcements from the city of Slonim, accompanied by a few tanks and vehicles full of German soldiers, were blocked by the partisans who were waiting for them on both sides of the roadway in ambush positions. These partisans fired at them from all directions and forced the German units to retreat with many casualties.

There was great satisfaction at the general staff and headquarters of all the partisans operating in Belorussia. The news of this victory also reached the general population in the surrounding villages and towns.

◊ ◊ ◊

When news of this decisive partisan victory reached the Germans and their collaborators, all feeling of security and superiority was lost. Now the Germans understood that they were dealt serious blows from strong forces that were willing to sacrifice themselves in order to take revenge for the murders of their loved ones.

After that battle, the Germans dug trenches in their remaining strongholds and sat in them in fear. The Germans would only venture out in large forces with tanks.

The acknowledgement of this humiliation was very difficult for the Germans to accept. The Jewish partisans, with great courage, willingness and determination, accomplished the defeat of the German stronghold. Up until this point, the Germans regarded themselves highly and without question as superior and undefeatable.

GERMANS ELIMINATED IN DOBROFKA VILLAGE

As the fighting strength of the partisans in the forest of Pouchtcha Lipichanite increased, the task of cleaning up the surrounding areas from the Germans and their collaborators was beginning. The partisans needed to gain complete control of the surrounding villages and not allow the Germans near any of those areas. This was not an easy task.

In the beginning of October 1942, a large force of German units with forty vehicles managed to cross the Yeman River. The Germans reached the village of Dobrofka, which was close to the forest controlled by the partisans. The German forces took positions all over the village and proceeded to shoot the Gentile farmers and burn down their homes with their wives and children inside. The Germans showed no mercy to these villagers who had supported the partisans.

A large force of partisans set out towards the village to save the remaining villagers and to attack the German forces and cut off their retreat. When the Germans realized that they were surrounded by large units of partisans, they retreated in panic. The partisans went after the retreating Germans and wiped out many of them.

ATTACK ON GERMANS IN NAKRISHUK VILLAGE

Nakrishuk was a few miles from the forest and was in complete control of the partisans. A large number of Germans entered Nakrishuk in order to murder the farmers and to burn down their homes with their families inside. It was standard operating procedure by the Germans to punish villages that supported the partisans.

When the Germans approached the village, there were only three partisans there. All three attempted to deter the Germans from entering the village. The leader of the partisans immediately ordered one of the partisans to get on his horse and inform the partisan company of the approaching Germans. The two remaining partisans exchanged fire with the Germans in order to stall them until the rest of the partisans could join the battle.

The two partisans fought until one was killed and the other was wounded. The wounded partisan shot himself with his own revolver so as not to fall into the hands of the Germans.

A large force of partisans arrived and separated into two units. One unit was to cut off the retreating Germans from the village, while the other unit went into the village to attack the Germans and a Latvian police unit. The second partisan unit successfully managed to force the Germans and Latvian police to retreat. As they retreated, they came into contact with the first partisan unit waiting in an ambush position. There were many casualties inflicted upon the Germans and Latvians.

The partisans returned victoriously to their base camp in the forest. However, their feelings of satisfaction were mixed with deep sorrow for the loss of the two partisans who fought courageously to stall the Germans advance into the village.

GERMANS FORCED OUT OF NAKRISHUK AGAIN

After the first battle in Nakrishuk that drove out the Germans, the Germans returned to the village for the second time to set up a stronghold. The village was heavily fortified with mine fields and artillery. The Zhetel Company, together with a unit of the Russian Burba Battalion, went out to attack and destroy the stronghold.

The partisan unit set out in April 1943 with a light tank in the lead. When the partisan forces reached the village, the order was given for the tank to open fire on the German stronghold. The partisans followed up with attacks on the Germans from all sides. The Germans retreated with heavy losses.

AMBUSH ON THE ROAD BETWEEN KUPITCH AND RHUDA YAVARSKI

In May 1943, a Zhetel Company platoon, aided by a small group of Russian partisans from the Orlanski Battalion, set up an ambush on the main road that led to the village of Rhuda

Yavarski. This road was the passageway for Germans to transport supplies to their strongholds in Rhuda Yavarski and other villages. The partisans took up positions on both sides of the road, about one third of a mile from the village, and awaited the arrival of the Germans.

At about six o'clock in the morning, two riders on horses were sent down the road to report if there was any approaching movement. They spotted a convoy of German vehicles and quickly returned to inform the partisans to get ready. As the convoy approached, one of the Russian partisans prematurely fired a shot, alerting the Germans, then some distance away.

The Germans jumped from their vehicles and took up positions on the side of the road to return fire. The partisans opened fire and managed to subdue the Germans and caused them to flee, with the exception of the German commander who managed to hide behind a large rock with a sniper rifle. The German was able to kill one of the partisan commanders. The partisans also suffered a few wounded.

PARTISAN HOSPITAL INFILTRATED BY A SPY

As the number of partisans grew and their main activities and battles increased, it became necessary to establish a medical unit to provide first aid and to take care of the sick and wounded. It was not possible to continue in the same manner as before, when there were fewer numbers of wounded who could be left behind to be helped by hiding in friendly villages. Now, with the larger battles, there were many more wounded to attend to.

Headquarters gave the order to build a hospital deep in a forest where there were many swamps. The hospital would be located between Rhuda Lipichanka and Vasespich. A route was established through the dense swamp and sand marshes to a location where the hospital was quickly built. It was well hidden from the Germans in a place that was difficult to find. Every battalion provided a few partisans to run the hospital, some for protection, and others for services and medical staff.

The hospital consisted of four huts. The Jewish partisans managed the hospital. Doctors Miesnick, Alperta and Recover were well-known as courageous fighters among the partisans. The morale of the partisans was high as they now felt that the action taken by their high command to care for the sick and wounded was a very significant commitment.

◊ ◊ ◊

During the summer of 1943, the Germans attempted to infiltrate the partisans by placing an attractive Russian woman among the partisans. The Germans expected that she would provide them with information on the location of the partisan hospital so they could destroy it. They almost succeeded.

When she arrived in the forest, she was interviewed by the headquarters' commander. She claimed to have escaped from a prisoner's train and that her will was to join the partisans in their struggle. She also claimed that she was a nurse and could therefore be very helpful in aiding the recovery of the wounded partisans.

As a nurse, she was sent to the hospital where she worked hard day and night, earning the trust of the partisans. She paid great attention to each and every wounded partisan by speaking to them and asking them all kinds of questions. One wounded partisan became very suspicious of her line of questioning. She wanted to know the exact details of his battles and how he became wounded. He reported his suspicions to the head of the hospital command.

The partisan command decided to follow her movements and behavior and to make inquires about her among the other partisans. She was summoned to the headquarters to be questioned. She broke down and admitted having been sent by the Germans. She and forty other women took a special course in Minsk on spying. Her mission was to find the location of the partisan hospital and to serve as a spy for the Germans.

The partisans retrieved as much information as possible from her regarding other such spies, as well as information on other German collaborators. In the end she was executed.

The Germans had failed in their attempt to locate the partisan hospital.

PARTISAN DEMOLITION ACTIVITIES

After a few successful battles, the partisans captured and accumulated explosive supplies. Their actions against the Germans expanded. They now had men with extensive mine demolition expertise to blow up railways, bridges and vehicles. Their goal was to disrupt any transportation of supplies from reaching the eastern Russian front and in turn, shorten the war.

On a daily basis, others came from Moscow to the partisan headquarters to strengthen demolition activities and to destroy communication and transportation facilities. The Zhetel

Company succeeded in their tasks under their commander, Israel Bushel. He had the responsibility for carrying out many dozens of railroad destructions.

Bushel was technically astute and had expert and extensive knowledge of mines. His name was well-known throughout the partisan community of Belorussia. He designed a mine, which the Germans were unable to disarm without setting it off. This newly designed mine brought panic among the Germans.

◊ ◊ ◊

The partisan demolition team managed to destroy hundreds of trains filled with supplies, ammunition and German soldiers. Dozens of bridges were blown up. The Germans tried everything possible to combat these demolition units without success. They attempted to operate the trains at a slower speed so that fewer cars would be destroyed, in case the train ran over a mine. The Germans even cleared all of the trees and bushes along both sides of the railway in order to deter the partisans. However, this was not enough to stop the demolition team. The struggle against the Germans continued.

One night, the Germans ambushed Bushel and his men while they were placing a mine under a bridge. With the approach of the German vehicles, Bushel noticed that the Germans outnumbered the partisans. There was insufficient time to allow for the connection of the mine to the electric wire, which would set it off remotely. Bushel did not want to risk the failure of the mission and decided to send all of his men back and blow up the bridge on his own, together with all of the Germans and their vehicles. He died a hero in doing so.

Posthumously, he received the highest medal possible – "Hero of the Soviet Union."

◊ ◊ ◊

There were many other successful Jewish partisan demolition units from other towns and villages. There was Baruch Levine from the town of Jaludok, Benjamin Baron from Lida and others. Heroic activities were also carried out by Zhetel partisans. Eli Kovinski was also awarded a medal, "Hero of the Soviet Union." He lost his arm in battle. Under heavy fire from a fortified German bunker, he volunteered to approach the bunker single handedly and throw in a bunch of grenades, which killed seventeen Germans and wounded four. His actions saved many partisan lives.

Two seventeen year old boys from Zhetel, Aralle Hidekofski and Shlomele Eskovitch, carried out many demolition duties. They destroyed a train loaded with German soldiers on the west side of the Neman River, an area known where Polish bandits operated. The Polish bandits ambushed these two youngsters, who fought to the very end and died heroically. They were posthumously awarded the medal, "The Red Star," for their courage and loyalty to the struggle against the German enemy.

The murder of these two boys from Zhetel was not to be forgotten. The partisan headquarters planned an action of revenge against the Polish anti-Semitic bandits. The order was given to stop them once and for all from continuing their activities. A large number of partisans crossed the Neman River and wiped all of them out for good.

THE GERMANS HUNT FOR PARTISANS

It was during the winter of 1942 on a cold December day when an attack of artillery fire from the main highway and other areas began. There were even bombardments from the air. The Lenin Brigade partisans, along with civilians, were in their winter *zemlyankas.* These shelters were cleverly camouflaged and had disguised entrances and exits.

The Lenin Brigade partisans immediately prepared for battle. As previously planned, each battalion and brigade took up their positions in case an attack took place. One battalion was sent to block off the main highway from the town of Derechim through the Schara River towards the forest. The other battalions took up ambush positions along the length of the River Neman. Three Jewish platoons from Zhetel assumed their positions on the main road leading to the Poushtcha forest. A few partisans remained to guard the camp.

The first platoon from Zhetel took up a position along the main road connecting the village of Rhuda Yavarski to the town of Kazlochena. The second platoon was positioned on the road leading from Zhetel to the village of Rapischa. The third platoon took its position along the road that led from the village of Nakrishuk to the partisan camp and the camps of the families that were hiding in the Poushtcha forest. In this manner, all of the fighting units organized a defense against the German attack on the Poushtcha Lipichanite forest, where the partisan stronghold was situated.

When the battle against the German forces began, all the partisans, particularly the Jewish partisans, fought heroically for two weeks against the superior German forces. The Germans were armed with tanks, artillery and fighter aircraft. Nevertheless, the partisans managed to inflict very heavy casualties upon the German enemy. But the Jewish partisans also suffered many fatalities; each partisan death was considered a great loss.

The first platoon fought a long battle to prevent the advance of heavily armed German mobile units from reaching the forest, until they ran out of ammunition. Before deciding on an orderly retreat, a messenger was dispatched to partisan headquarters to inform them of the situation.

Three Jewish partisans volunteered to save the only artillery they had from falling into German hands. The area where the artillery was located had already been overrun by the German forces. The remaining members of the partisan platoon provided cover fire for the volunteers who attempted to retrieve the artillery piece. During this battle, the partisans lost their leader, Hershel Kaplinsky.

According to my Cousin Kalman's account, it was Hershel Kaplinsky, together with my father, who led Kalman and his brother, Moyshele, and his mother, Batya, along with twelve other Jewish men, out of hiding in the attic of the synagogue in Zhetel and to safety in the forest.

Two other partisan platoons fought against the German advance until the partisans finally had to retreat. To avoid discovery by the advancing Germans, the platoons divided themselves into smaller groups and retreated deep into the Pouschtcha swamps and forest. There they organized an offensive of hit and run battles to fight against the much larger German forces. During this retreat, a small unit of partisans came up against a large German unit that had managed to infiltrate deep into the forest. A battle ensued until the partisans eliminated the German unit.

The Germans were now afraid to enter the forest because of possible ambushes. The siege by the Germans lasted over three weeks. The Germans set fire to the villages around the forest and murdered many of the farmers for helping the partisans.

When the German attack began, many of the civilian families had to leave their well-camouflaged *zemlyankas*, which were already prepared for the winter. The civilians escaped quickly, taking very little with them in the hope that the siege would not last long. They roamed from place to place, cold and hungry, some with small children. Many of the civilians suffered from frostbite, typhus, rashes, fevers, and lice. Weakened, many fell into German hands and were murdered.

After three weeks, the Germans started to move their forces back to the eastern front. They realized that fighting the partisans in the forest was too difficult because there were too many unknowns and fighting in unknown terrain gave the advantage to the partisans. The Germans decided they could not tie up so many resources just to deal with the partisans.

The partisans all felt relieved as they were now able to go about the forest more freely, taking care of the wounded and the ill, and cleaning themselves and their clothing. The families of the partisans returned to their camps in the Nakrishuk and Puzyestz forests.

The partisans became even stronger when many of the farmers and peasants, whose homes had been destroyed by the Germans, came to the forest to join up with them.

The families of the partisans did not rest. They went out in convoys to find new supplies of food, horses and wagons to re-establish the strength of the partisan units.

THE LIBERATION OF THE PARTISANS

In the early part of July 1944, the Germans once again surrounded and attacked the forest with a large army of Russian and Ukrainian collaborators. They burned down the remaining villages and farms and murdered many peasants for helping the partisans. They also distributed propaganda leaflets to convince the partisans to surrender. This time, the partisans were far stronger than in the past and were able the fight the Germans with great success.

It was now the middle of summer and much easier for the partisan families to hide underground. Once the hiding places were covered with trees and other camouflage, it was almost impossible for the Germans to find them. The partisan fighters and civilians knew from previous experience to prepare themselves with larger quantities of food and water.

Our families spent almost an entire month underground. There were only a few short times we went out at night during that month. We sensed that the end of the Germans was near and that we would eventually be liberated by the Russian army. That day finally arrived.

My Cousin Kalman describes his experience when our families were liberated:

"On September 7, 1944, early in the morning, we heard movement of an army of soldiers and horses. We took our chances that this time it was the Russian army and not the Germans or their collaborators retreating through the forest. We anxiously approached the soldiers. We wanted to meet the first Russian liberators. When we reached them, we hugged and kissed them and cried. We told the Russian soldiers that many of us were murdered and never lived to be free, and to see the end of the Nazis." [2, 3]

APPENDIX A

SIGNIFICANT EVENTS IN ZHETEL HISTORY

The following are significant events that occurred after the initial German invasion of Zhetel on September 1, 1939. These dates are based on historical information.

Date	Significant Events In Zhetel
September 1, 1939	German Army invades Poland.
June 30, 1941	Nazi's enter, capture and occupy Zhetel.
July 14, 1941	All Jews ordered to wear Yellow Star of David.
July 15, 1941	First six Jews murdered in Zhetel.
July 23, 1941	Nazi's execute 120 prominent Jewish people of Zhetel.
October 1, 1941	German Task Force arrives to implement "Final Solution."
November 1941	Alter Dvoretsky forms partisan resistance group.
December 15, 1941	Germans take 400 Jews to Dvoretz forced labor camp. Dvoretz is about 10-12 km from Zhetel.
February 22, 1942	All Jews in Zhetel are rounded up and ordered into a ghetto, fenced in by wire.

Date	Significant Events In Zhetel
April 30, 1942	Mass murder of 1000 Jewish residents. All Jews hunted down and killed. Some of the Jewish residents escape and flee to the forest.
May 11, 1942	Alter Dvoretzky, prominent elder and partisan commander, murdered in the forest by Russian Army deserters.
August 6, 1942	Final liquidation of Zhetel Jewish population.
July 7, 1944	Remaining Jewish survivors liberated from the forests by the Soviet Army.
August 1944	Returning to their homes after the war, the indigenous population makes it clear to Jewish Holocaust survivors that they are not welcome and will not be tolerated in Belorussia anymore. Thus, the survivors become refugees in their own country. Jewish survivors begin a six-month trek by foot, horse and railroad to Displaced Persons Camps in Europe for passage to Israel, the United States, Canada, and other countries.

Date	Significant Events **Shlamke and Shanke Minuskin and Their Children Leave Zhetel**
May 1945	By way of Zhetel and Poland, Shlamke and Shanke Minuskin, and their children, Henikel and Kalmanke, enter Frankfurt *am Main* (on the Main River) Displaced Persons Camp, and then on to Zeilsheim, Germany.
September 6, 1946	The Minuskin family leaves Port of Bremen, Germany, aboard the steamship Marine Marlin, en route to the U.S.A.
September 16, 1946	The Minuskin family arrives in the Port of New York.
May 1952	The Minuskin family, now named Sam, Sonia, Harold, and Carl, become American citizens.

APPENDIX B

PHOTOGRAPHS AND DOCUMENTS

Some of the following pictures and documents were sent to relatives in the United States before the war; others were found after the war. Additionally, some were taken during my family's journey from Belorussia to the United States.

The names may be awkward to the English speaking reader. Since we spoke Yiddish, among other languages, we all had Yiddish names. My mother was *Shanke*. In Yiddish *Shanke* means beautiful. My father was called *Shlamke*. I was named after my mother's father, *Henach*, but I was called *Henikel*. My brother, *Kalmanke,* was named after my father's father, *Kalman*. My first cousin, *Kalman*, about whom stories are told in this book, was also named after our grandfather.

When we arrived in the United States, we tried to become more "Americanized." My mother's name was changed to Sonia and my father became Sam. I became Harold and my brother Carl, respectively.

Harold Minuskin

Shanke Orlinsky, ca.1930s.

Hinde Leah Orlinsky, Rifkeh Rochel Orlinsky
(their mother) and Shanke Orlinsky, ca. 1920s.

Shlamke Minuskin (on the left) with his bicycle friends, ca. 1920s.

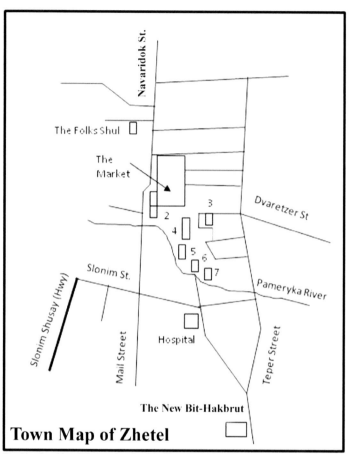

Town Map of Zhetel

2. Catholic Church, 3. Folks Bank, 4. New Bet-Shmedres,
5. Old & Middle Bet-Shmedres, 6. Bank, 7. Talmud Tayreh.
Ref. Town Plan of Zhetel,
prepared by Rubin Mitsky from Pinsky's Zhetel.[4]

150

Shlamke and Shanke Minuskin in their
backyard garden in Zhetel, ca. 1937.

Shlamke and Shanke Minuskin in their backyard in Zhetel, ca. 1937.

"The Palace" in Zhetel, the hospital where Shanke Minuskin gave birth to Henikel, and about two years later to Kalmanke, ca. 1938.

Shlamke, Henikel and Shanke in the family home backyard in Zhetel, ca. 1939.

A group of partisans from the Lenin Brigade in which Shlamke
Minuskin served as a weapons specialist, ca 1942-1944.

Areas of Partisan Operations, 1942 to 1944

156

Some of the survivors from Zhetel pose in 1945. On the left, first row, Henikel Minuskin is sitting between his parents, Shlamke and Shanke. Kalmanke is held by his father, Shlamke.

Shanke, Kalmanke and Henikel Minuskin in
their winter coats that they wore in the forests.
Shanke sewed the children's coats from one
captured German army coat, ca. 1945.

Passover Seder in1945 near Frankfurt, Germany.
Starting 3rd from left, Shlamke, Kalmanke,
Henikel and Shanke Minuskin.

Passover Seder in 1945 near Frankfurt, Germany. On the left are Shlamke, Shanke, Kalmanke, and Henikel Minuskin, together with the extended family of survivors from Zhetel.

The extended family of survivors from Zhetel. Fifth and sixth from the left are Shanke and Shlamke Minuskin. Henikel is in front of Shlamke. Kalmanke is standing in front on the right, ca. 1945, near Frankfurt, Germany.

Shanke Minuskin (on the right) with a friend
at the temporary family home in Zeilsheim,
Germany, ca. 1945.

Shanke Minuskin (on the right)
with her friend, Sonke Mordkowsky,
Zeilsheim, Germany, ca. 1945.

The Minuskin family in Zeilsheim,
Germany, ca. 1945.

Kalmanke (foreground) and Henikel in the backyard of the temporary family home in Zeilsheim, Germany, near the DP camp, ca. 1945.

Left to right, Kalmanke, Shlamke, Henikel, Shlamik (behind the wheel) and Zavel Mordkowsky by their truck in Zeilsheim, Germany, ca. 1945.

A picnic in the countryside near the DP camp. Shlamke Minuskin is standing dressed in his partisan uniform. Kalmanke and Henikel are at the bottom foreground, ca.1945.

Some of the Zhetel survivors at an outing near
the DP camp. Shanke Minuskin is in the
foreground and Henikel is at the bottom, ca. 1945.

Shlamke Minuskin's Russian driver's license, 2nd class, which permitted him to drive any kind of vehicle, ca.1944.

This is a Provisional identity paper issued to Shanke Minuskin, indicating that she was a civilian serving in the army as a seamstress in the Partisan 3rd Region Regiment No. 01397, ca. 1945.

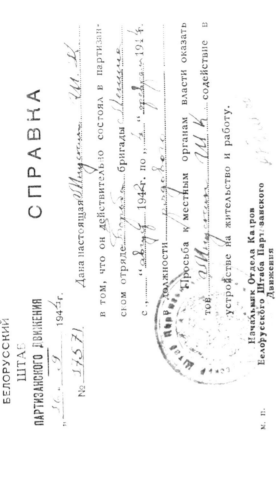

This identifies that Shlamke Minuskin (Shlema Kalmovich Minuskin) served with the Partisan Detachment of the Lenin Brigade from August 1942 to February 1944. The document appeals to the authorities to provide him housing and employment.

Henikel, Kalmanke and Shanke Minuskin
(their mother) in Warsaw. The Polish Army
is marching in the background, ca. 1945.

Henikel, Shlamke (their father) and
Kalmanke in Warsaw, ca. 1945.

This is the Minuskin family vaccination certificate. The service was performed by the United Nations Relief and Rehabilitation Administration (UNRRA) doctors on August 21, 1946.

HIAS: The Hebrew Immigrant Aid
Society button that the Minuskin family wore
upon departure from Bremen, Germany
en route to the U.S.A.

Henikel's (Harold's) identity
photo for entry into the U.S.A.

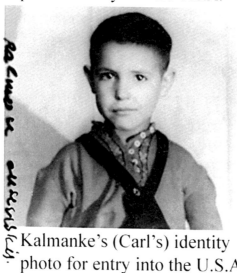

Kalmanke's (Carl's) identity
photo for entry into the U.S.A.

Minuskin family portrait for the
identity papers to enter the U.S.A.,
ca. 1946.

The Minuskin family identity papers for
entry into the U.S.A. on September 16, 1946.

177

The University of the State of New York

THE STATE EDUCATION DEPARTMENT

DUPLICATE Nº 257386

TO BE KEPT BY APPLICANT

Sonia Minureir
[Sign your name on this line]

150 E 182 st Bronx
[Address: Number and Street]

New York N.Y.
[City] [Zone]

Be it Known that the person whose name and address are entered herein, having met the requirements prescribed in Section 166 of the Election Law, and rules and regulations of the Regents of the State of New York, and having made the signature appearing herein in the presence of the examiner, is herewith granted a CERTIFICATE OF LITERACY.

[Place of Examination: School] Bronx [Borough] [Date] 19
[Examiner's Signature] [File No.]

William Jansen
Superintendent of Schools

Commissioner of Education

NOTICE TO ELECTION INSPECTORS. This Duplicate Certificate of Literacy is not valid for registration. It is to be kept by the applicant as evidence of having fulfilled the literacy requirement for new voters.

The University of the State of New York

THE STATE EDUCATION DEPARTMENT

ORIGINAL Nº 257386

GIVE TO ELECTION INSPECTOR

Sonia Minureir
[Sign your name on this line]

150 E 182 st Bronx
[Address: Number and Street]

New York N.Y.
[City] [Zone]

Be it Known that the person whose name and address are entered herein, having met the requirements prescribed in Section 166 of the Election Law, and rules and regulations of the Regents of the State of New York, and having made the signature appearing herein in the presence of the examiner, is herewith granted a CERTIFICATE OF LITERACY.

[Place of Examination: School] Bronx [Borough] [Date] 19
[Examiner's Signature] [File No.]

William Jansen
Superintendent of Schools

Commissioner of Education

This original Certificate of Literacy must be handed to the election inspector.

Shanke's (Sonia's) certificate for English proficiency that was issued in 1952.

178

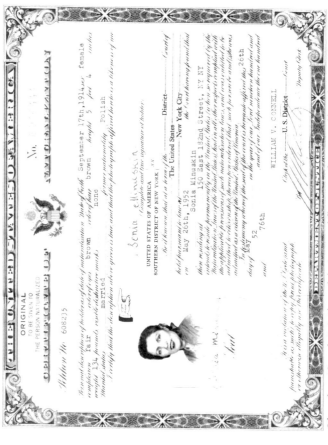

Shanke (Sonia) Minuskin's certificate of naturalization. Shanke went to night school to learn English. She became a U.S. citizen in May 1952.

Shanke (Sonia) Minuskin's citizenship
photograph taken in early 1952.

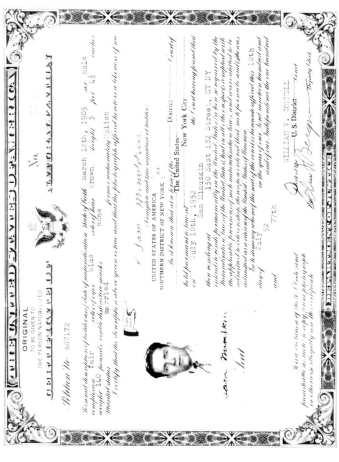

Shlamke (Sam) Minuskin went to night school to learn English so he could become a U.S. citizen in July 1952.

181

Shanke Minuskin, right foreground, with relatives in Kvar Saba, Israel. Kalman Minuskin, Shanke's nephew is 3rd from the left, ca. 1953.

Kalman Minuskin, ca. 1960s.

Cousin Kalman Minuskin and family, ca. 1960s.

Shanke (Sonia) and Shlamke (Sam) Minuskin
in New York, ca. 1955.

APPENDIX C

FAMILY NAMES

The following list represents some of the Minuskin family members from the town of Zhetel who survived by escaping from the Germans and living in the forests with the partisans.

Henikel (Harold) Minuskin: The older son of Shanke and Shlamke. He translated and annotated his mother's memoirs from Yiddish to English.
Kalmanke (Carl) Minuskin: The younger son of Shanke and Shlamke.
Shanke (Sonia) Minuskin: Henikel's and Kalmanke's mother. Shanke in Yiddish means beautiful. Died November 2008.
Shlamke (Sam) Minuskin: Father of Henikel and Kalmanke. He fought with the partisans. Died August 1984.

◊ ◊ ◊

Kalman Minuskin: First cousin of Henikel and Kalmanke. He immigrated to Israel after the war. Died August 2008.
Myarim Minuskin: Shlamke's oldest brother and Kalman's father
Batya Minuskin: Kalman's mother and Myarim's wife
Moshele Minuskin: Kalman's younger brother
Mulke Minuskin: Shlamke's brother and another Kalman's father
Yoche Minuskin: Mulke's wife and the other Kalman's mother
Mirel and Kalman Minuskin: Mulke's and Yoche's two children

Laybke Minuskin, my father's younger brother, escaped from Zhetel by train to eastern Russian and survived the war, immigrating to the United States when my parents sponsored him in the late 1940s. Nyomke (Benjamin) Minuskin, the youngest of my father's brothers, immigrated to Israel before the war.

◊ ◊ ◊

The following members of my immediate family perished in Zhetel at the hands of the Germans.

Dvora Minuskin: Shlamke Minuskin's mother
Friedka Minuskin: Shlamke Minuskin's sister
Barrele Minuskin: Kalman Minuskin's younger brother
Shepsele Minuskin: Kalman Minuskin's younger brother

◊ ◊ ◊

Rivkeh Rochel Orlinsky: Shanke Minuskin's mother
Leib Orlinsky: Shanke Minuskin's brother
Rikleh Orlinsky: Wife of Leib Orlinsky and Shanke's sister-in-law
Chanah Orlinsky: Shanke's 20 year old niece
Raiseleh Orlinsky: Shanke's 17 year old niece
Payke Orlinsky: Shanke's 14 year old nephew
Henachke Orlinsky: Shanke's 6 year old nephew

◊ ◊ ◊

And others whose names are lost to history.

GLOSSARY

The following words and definitions will serve as a guide to help English speaking readers understand the terms and expressions used in these memoirs.

ablaveh (Russian): to trap, or to set a trap; a very thorough search, as to set up an ablaveh to catch wolves. The word was used by the partisans to characterize a major raid by the Germans into the forest in an effort to capture and kill Jews.

atraid (Russian): regiment, a partisan fighting unit

aytzeh (Yiddish): a way out, a solution

bah-shefenesh (Hebrew): a sub-human creature

bahynk (Yiddish): long (for)

balabosteym (Yiddish): homemakers

bashert (Yiddish): so willed, so it will be

Belorussian (Belarus): relating to Belarus (current name) or its people language, or culture

boychikez (Yiddish): young men, or older boys

Displaced Persons (DP) Camp: A place where many Holocaust survivors found temporary lodging, food, medical treatment, and schooling for their children after the war.

ehtizhe (Yiddish): a plan, or a solution

eingshaft (Yiddish): crowded conditions of people

farfehl (Yiddish): small pellet-shaped noodles

fraylach (Yiddish): happy, lively

geleger (Yiddish): sleeping place

geroy (Russian): hero

goiyishe (Yiddish): gentile, used as an adjective

Goyim (Yiddish): gentiles; non-Jews, sometimes used to refer to peasants

haminke chalochim (Yiddish-Hebrew): dreams about home

hoben zeh befallen (Yiddish):attacked them

ibergekerte (Yiddish): turned upside down

Jueden Rayn (German): clean out the Jews

kapore hindele (Hebrew): sacrificial chicken

Katyusha rocket (Russian): a multiple rocket launcher; a type of rocket artillery fielded by the former Soviet Union in WW II

klozeh (Yiddish): a toilet, or an outhouse

Kristallnacht (German): The Night of Broken Glass

kropoveh (Yiddish-Russian): a plant with leaves like poison ivy; causes itching when in contact with the skin

latke (Yiddish): pancake

mazel (Yiddish-Hebrew: luck

mechaye (Yiddish-Hebrew): pleasure

mentshen (Yiddish): people, adults

mishpoche (Yiddish-Hebrew): family or relatives

nakeim (Hebrew): sorry

na Sabir (Russian): towards Siberia, heading towards Siberia

nekome (Hebrew): revenge

Nemetski (Russian): German

onyetzeh (Yiddish): a rag

partisan(s) (Yiddish-Russian): resistance fighter(s) who fought against the Germans and their collaborators in World War II

peltz (Yiddish): a fur or a pelt, at times used to line a winter coat *piroshkehs* (Polish): honey covered pastries with poppy seeds

pogram(Yiddish-Russian): an organized massacre of helpless people

schlepping (Yiddish): carrying

Shabbos (Yiddish-Hebrew): the Sabbath, the day of rest

shmutz (Yiddish) filth

shtait kapayreh (Yiddish): disheveled, wild, like hair

shtetl (Yiddish): town of 1000 to 5000 people, mostly Jewish

shusay (Russia): main road or highway

shvacher neffeshly (Yiddish-Hebrew): weak soul

Sondefüehrer (German): a special leader; a German military appointment for former enemy territories that had been "liberated" by the Germans

tzorehs (Yiddish): troubles

yontovim (Yiddish-Hebrew): holidays

zemlyanka (Russian): an underground dwelling or shelter used by civilians and partisans during WW II in the Belorussian forests; derived from the Russian word for "dugout"

zetik (Yiddish): nourishing

FOOTNOTES

[1]Eliach, Yaffa, *There Once Was a World* (Little Brown and Company, 1998, pp 561-562, pp 629-630).

[2]Minuskin, Kalman, *In the Ghetto and In the Forest*, (Kvar Saba, Israel: Self published, 1990). (Hebrew)

[3]Minuskin, Galit, *In the Ghetto and In the Forest*, (Kvar Saba, Israel; Self published, 1990, Translated from Hebrew into English, 1992).

[4]Kaplinski, Baruch, *Pinkas Zetel*, (Tel-Aviv, Israel: Zetel Association, 1957). (Yiddish)

[5]Kahanovich, Moshe, *Der Yidisher onteyl in der partizaner-bavegung fun Sovet-Rusland*, (Rome and New York, 1948). (Yiddish)

[6]Bessonov, Evgeni, *Tank Rider: Into the Reich with the Red Army,* (London: Greenhill Books; Pennsylvania: Stackpole Books, 2003).